Blessings,
Jacqueline

Juan's Story

A True Story

Jacqueline Boatwright

Juan's Story

PUBLISHED BY
JACQUELINE BOATWRIGHT
2572 LINCOLNTON PARKWAY
HEPHZIBAH, GA 30815

Website address: anthonydejuan.com

Scripture taken from the
New King James Version, Copyright 1982

ISBN 0-9725295-0-0

Copyright © 2002 by Jacqueline Boatwright

All rights reserved. No parts of this book may be reproduced or transmitted in any form or by any means, electronic or mechanical, including photocopying and recording, or by any information storage and retrieval system, without permission in writing from the publisher.

Printed in the United States of America
2002 – First Edition
Quality Printing, North Augusta, SC

In Dedication

I dedicate this book to my loving mother, Coriene Boatwright. I am so happy that your spirit taught me how to forgive from my heart.

My friends Shelia and Wayne Scarber, Debbie Williams, Frances Burwell, Gary and Patsy Hillman, Kevin Bowles, Dot Sapp, Jennifer Taylor, Theracia Prescott and Shirley Newton, thank you all for your kindness and your encouragement.

To Richard Ingram, thank you for your patience, your unselfishness, your dedication to my cause and giving of your time and expertise. You are one of the most wonderful men I have ever met. I will never forget you, and all you have done for my family and me.

To Greg Rickabaugh, thank you for writing such beautiful stories about my baby and all that we have endured.

The same goes for Timothy Cox, I appreciate you.

To Phil Wasson, thanks for giving 911 the heads up on Juan and for your editing contribution to this book.

To the Augusta, GA, Fire Department, Engine Company 18, Juan is still your baby.

To the Rural Metro Ambulance, EMT's and Paramedics, you did a super job at saving Juan's life, twice.

To the Augusta/Rural Metro 911 dispatchers, you are appreciated by the Boatwright Family.

To my brothers, and my sisters, thank you for your support.

To Adrian and Dereck, I love you with all my heart.

To the nurses that took such wonderful care of Juan I truly hope that God Bless each of you in a special way.

To the television and radio media that gave us such gracious coverage, especially Leon Moore, thank you.

To Crystal Boggs, you will always hold a special place in my heart, I love you and God Bless you.

To P. Kone, my heart will always be open to you for I could never repay you for everything you have brought into our lives. Thank you.

To Bianca and Miriam, thank you for your love, donations, and your friendship.

To the citizens of Grovetown, Georgia, thank you for your generosity.

To my Precious Nellie, you have been there for me and I will always love you for it.

To my Pastor, Alan Webb and Church Family, Johnson Chapel Baptist, thank you for loving us spiritually.

To all those who said prayers or sent kind words, although I may not have called your name, please know that I deeply appreciate you for all you have done, given, or said to help us along the way.

And last but most certainly above all things here on earth, My Lord and Savior Jesus Christ, thank you for looking beyond my faults and seeing my needs.

Forever,
Jackie

To

Robin Henderson Danforth

Thank you.

May you forever rest in peace.

To All the Women Who Dared To Make A Difference.
Forever Jacqueline

I Am Woman
(written 2000)

Being a woman is the best thing that could have ever happened to me. I learned through countless trials and tribulations that loving me, respecting me, protecting me and being the best me I could be was the best thing I could do for me.

The hardest time of my life brought true meaning to the old gospel adage, "joy comes in the morning." I have learned to be grateful and appreciative to the things and people in my life that while sometimes living in this world, I often took for granted. More than that, I realized that to succeed in life I had to stop negative patterns, stop doing hurtful things to myself and to others.

Learning and understanding my woman hood was a great challenge. Appreciating it was even more of a challenge. After being devastated in a past relationship, I had to find ways to heal my pain and to love those who for some unknown reason chose to hurt me. I realized that sometimes, you out grow people, things, and even situations. I just decided to be happy. I refused to allow situations, people or things to interrupt my happiness.

I truly understand my empowerment as a woman, a single mother, a lover and a friend. I decided to only do what is expected of me, not what others expect. I allow myself to laugh, take life slow and enjoy the simple pleasures that for so long I have rushed by.

I am forever thankful for God's grace and his mercy. So many times when I cried and felt all alone it was that grace and mercy that kept me strong and gave me the extra boost I needed to get through another day. I am stronger than ever in my faith, because I know it gives me hope for tomorrow. My family is a priority, for they keep me grounded and give me reasons for setting and achieving goals.

By loving my self I have definitely increased my ability to give and receive love. I have learned to take care of me physically and mentally. I've educated my self and embarked on a mission. I have been, dumped, physically and verbally abused. Yet I still love and appreciate the black man. I know that even though I love my children, my family and my man, happiness is an individual thing. I have made mistakes with relationships: throughout the mistakes, I know I did my best. I will not allow the ugly to stop me from seeing the beauty in what could be if the right two people connect.

So many times my fears stopped me from reaching my success, by undermining my dreams, hopes and aspirations. I now take those same fears and allow them to activate my efforts to expedite my potential to succeed. The pains and heartaches I suffered from being broken-hearted have become pains and aches of wisdom and courage to do better, be better, want more and have more. I truly understand who I am and that it is me and only me that make me what I am. My courage lies deeply embedded in my heart and soul; fertilized by suffering, pains, healing wounds and my greatest fears. My empowerment is what shapes and molds me as a woman, to be a great mother, a great friend, and a great lover.

I have spent so much time not knowing, not growing, not understanding and not being understood. Today, I stand proud and tall, thankful for the good and the bad, the wrong and the right. I promised me to be consistent with my courage, and to not spend the next year doing the same thing I did the year before. I promised me that I was going to reach a little farther, seek a little harder, speak a little louder and listen a little more carefully.

The woman in me will not allow me to give up or give out. Not because I was hurt, but because I was hurt: Not because I was angry, but because I was angry. I hope one can understand how needless fears and scars can, if not controlled, gain complete control of your destiny.

My inner strength allows me to reach out to others and encourage them to live beyond their front doors. To help them create in themselves today who they will be tomorrow. Be true to yourself first. I truly believe God gave us all a gift or calling; we have to reach inside and find it, live it, breathe it, believe it, and become it. I have been faced with many bad situations and had to make the decision to face it or run away. I decided to put my gloves on and fight for the chance to elevate my life. Running away from any situation does not solve it or help it, instead it only adds fuel to the flame. Nine times out of ten almost every situation could have been conquered: If I would have taken the time to think, subdue my fear or slow my anger.

I often dream and I am proud to be a dreamer. For if it was not for my dreams I could not visualize my goals. I teach my children that it is okay to dream, just wake up and make it a reality. I teach my children to be thankful and pray. For it is your spirituality that keeps you rooted on the right track in life.

I have been up and I have been down so low that I didn't think that I could muster up the strength to get up and get going again. I opted to reach toward the little voice in me that encouraged me not to stay down, but to get up and run wide open. If I wanted to cry along the way, I cried, if I wanted to scream I did that too. What ever it took to make my running not be in vain, I did.

I take pride in reaching back to enrich others through my obstacles, trials, joys and heartaches. It feels somewhat comforting to know that you are not alone in your struggles and when you hear the plight of others you sometimes realize your fight was not a war only just a battle.

My womanhood is God's way of telling me I made you strong, proud, smart and faithful. I realized that being a woman takes all of these and so much more. I know now that my true beauty lies in my heart, my giving, and in my spirit. It lies in sharing, in my caring, in my reaching and in my teaching. I am so proud to be a woman.

Chapter 1

September 9, 2001, what can I say about that day? It started out as a typical Sunday morning. I was getting ready to go to church. I decided to leave Juan, my 14-month-old son at his daycare. Juan was very active and after a period of sitting in one place, he would become agitated. How in the world, could I have ever known that this day would change my life forever?

I remember getting dressed and playing this gospel CD, watching in awe and spiritual laughter as Juan danced his little feet and clapped his hands, moving to the beat of the music.

"Go Juan! Go Juan!" I chanted and praised God along with him.

He is such a beautiful little boy, with perfectly rounded eyes that are so dark, my Mom says, "they look like deep dark holes in his head." He has two little teeth in the top of his mouth and a matching pair at the bottom, as he is dancing and smiling, I see his dimples. In complete joy at his rejoicing, I reached out, grabbed him and gave him a great big hug and kiss.

Suddenly I remembered that the bathtub water was running. I raced to the bathroom to turn the faucet off. I called to Juan and he came running, he loved to take a bath and splash water every where, including my face.

After his bath, I rubbed his little body down in lotion, I could not help but to steal a kiss every so often. His soft tiny face and hands tasted like honey, and the more kisses I gave him the more I wanted to give.

"You've got some sweet kisses Juan," I told him and he would always answer with the one phrase that he could articulate clearly, "Thank you!" That always got him a great big hug.

I called to Dereck, my 12 year-old, "Are you ready yet? It's time to go."

As I loaded Juan into his car seat, we headed a few houses down to his daycare. His little eyes stared at me with a look that I did not come to realize until a few hours later. I rang the doorbell, stealing Juan's sweet kisses as I waited for Maria, the day-care owner to answer.

Maria had kept Juan ever since he was about 3-months-old. I met her through a lady who was at Juan's pediatrician office. When she told me the location of the day care her baby was kept, my ears perked up. We live on the same street. She gave me the address and telephone number. The next day I went to see the place, it was clean, and other children were being dropped off as she was giving me a tour. She handed me forms to complete and showed me her state license. I liked her. She was young and we had many great conversations. Sometimes when I picked Juan up we would stand in her driveway talking for about an hour. She had three boys of her own; they all seemed to like Juan. They would follow us to the car playing with him as I loaded him in his car seat.

Maria's husband Monté, is a big, friendly guy, he helped Maria care for the children she kept. I remember times when I called back after dropping Juan off to check on him, Monté would be watching the children. I thought that was interesting.

He noticed my being anxious about his caring for my Juan and he would say, "Jackie, he is fine, I got everything under control."

"Where is Maria?" I asked. He would say she was at the grocery store or was gone to get her hair done. He was an adult and he was a part of their business, so what was I so worried about?

As Maria opened the door, with outstretched hands, she said to Juan, "Come here boy."

His little arms quickly and tightly grabbed me around my neck. She pulled him away and told him they were going to wake up her boys. I could hear him crying as I walked back to the car. I paused as I reached for the latch to open my car door. I started to go back in and get him, that moment changed everything for my family and me.

I got in the car and drove to South Carolina for church. As I walked through the church door, I saw babies everywhere and for some strange reason Juan's face seemed to appear on their bodies. I felt a little strange, but told myself I was just missing him. I heard a baby crying, the crying sounded so much like Juan, I asked if I could hold the baby. I wished in the deepest part of my heart that I had brought him with me, my longing was so strong, I could hardly wait for the service to end.

As the Pastor gave his soul stirring message entitled *"It's Your Move"* I could feel the presence of God inside me and my soul was filled with joy. The message was about how God is waiting to help us whenever we ask.

As the service neared its end, I leaned over and whispered in Dereck's ear, "We are going to stop for ice cream on the way home." That statement woke him up, he had slept through most of the service. As we left from the store eating our ice cream, I told Dereck that I could not wait to get Juan. I pressed on the gas pedal and began to focus my attention on getting home. At that same time, my cellular telephone rang. I answered it and my message waiting came into the display pad.

"Hello," I said.

It was Delma, Maria's sister, she and I had also become friends. We occasionally went out together and talked on the telephone a lot. We had been playing telephone tag for the past week and her call shocked me.

"Well, you can finally return my calls, huh? Are you at home?" I asked.

She replied, "No, I am at Fort Gordon."

"I guess you want me to come and pick you up?" I asked.

"Jackie, this isn't a pleasant call?" she said.

My heart fell deep and hard into my stomach as I humbly asked, "What have you all done to my baby?"

"Where are you?" She asked?

"I am on my way home from Edgefield, I was at church. What has happened to Juan?"

"Just come to Eisenhower Hospital, as soon as you can." she said.

"Is he alive?" I asked. Complete silence came and I lost it. I began to kick and scream, the car swerved on the road.

"Oh my God, Oh my God, my baby. Why did I leave my baby?"

I placed the telephone back to my ear, I could hear her asking me to calm down and reminding me I was driving. I begged her to tell me about Juan but she would not, I hung up the telephone and I wept from the inner most parts of my soul.

I felt as though my body was being forcefully crushed and it hurt me like no other pain I'd ever felt. I started placing calls to family members to let them know that something had happened to Juan. As I tried to regain control, I looked over at Dereck and the fear in his eyes made me realize I needed to get help, because I was losing it. It had begun to rain as we approached Augusta. Coupled with my tears and my heartache I lost all since of direction. I dialed 911.

I was crying so hard that my words were muffled and broken.

Finally the operator told me, "Ma'am, I can't understand you, stop crying, and tell me what is wrong."

As I attempted again to ask the 911 operator for a police officer to drive me to Eisenhower, I glanced up, and in front of me was a patrol car. I pulled up next to it, I felt so weak and numb. I asked Dereck to go inside and get the officer.

As the policewoman approached the car, I began to tell her about the telephone call I received about my baby and I asked her to drive me to the hospital where he was.

She asked, "Who placed this call to you, ma'am?"

I pressed the redial button on my telephone and handed it to her. After a short conversation, she asked me to park my car, and to get in the car with her. I took off my high-heeled shoes and ran in the rain to get into the patrol car. In the back of the police car, my head had become so heavy I could barely hold it up. I could taste my salted tears in my mouth. My body continued to ache and feel numb. My imagination began to take over. I thought what could have happened to him. Was he shot? Was he run over with the car? What?

My thoughts led me to call Maria's home with hopes that one of her children would answer and tell me what happened.

As I listened in anticipation of each ring, a man's voice said, "Hello."

"Monté, what has happened to Juan? You can tell me because I am not driving now and I need to know what happened to my baby."

"Is this Jackie?" the voice on the other end said.

"Monté, you know this is me, tell me what is wrong with Juan," I said.

"This is not Monté, this is the police investigator," answered the voice.

I screamed, "Oh my God, what is wrong with my baby? Tell me what happened."

He replied, "I can't, ma'am. Just get to Eisenhower as soon as you can."

I began to kick and scream all over again. I grabbed hold of Dereck and I wept until we got to the hospital.

As the officer came around to open the door, I quickly grabbed my purse and shoes and ran into the emergency room, asking anyone who looked as though they worked there, "Where is my baby?"

A lady sitting at the desk said, "You must be Ms. Boatwright. Come with me." I kept asking her to tell me what happened to my baby.

Her replies remained constant, "The doctor will come and tell you in a moment. Just wait here." I could tell by the look in her eyes that it was not good news.

As the doctor entered and sat next to me, he began to explain to me what had happened to Juan.

"It appears your son has suffered a near drowning accident from falling into a bucket of mop water containing bleach. He has been without a pulse for more than an hour but we have managed to get a heart beat. It is not a strong one right now but we have one."

For some reason, at that moment the only thing that mattered was my seeing him. "Can I see him?"

"Sure," he said, "but he has tubes in him so let me warn you."

As I entered the room. I could not see my son for the many white coats that stood closely around his bedside. Everything began to move and sound as though they were in slow motion. As the doctors and nurses peeled back one by one, to reveal Juan lying on the bed, I could feel the numbness running full speed up my legs until they felt as though they were not there and I collapsed. I was quickly brought back to my feet by two of the doctors as they asked if I were okay. I slowly walked toward the bed and grabbed my baby and his little body felt like a block of ice, he was not moving and he looked stiff. I laid my head next to his cheek and told him repeatedly how sorry I was for not taking him to church with me.

The doctors pulled me up, saying they had to get him prepared for transport to the Children's Medical Center. As I stood outside Juan's room, I asked for Maria. For some reason, I felt no anger or malice toward her, and I really wanted to tell her. The nurse told me that she was sedated, and in another room.

The ambulance ride from Eisenhower to the Children's Medical Center was just as unbelievable to me as was everything else I had witnessed. What was going on I thought? Why was this happening to me?

As they rushed Juan into the hospital, I held his little hand telling him, "Mommy is here sweetie, you hold on." I held his hand until they took him through the double doors. I leaned against the wall trying to gain the strength to stand as my body slid down to the floor. There I sat and wept. The inside of my body, hollow, I sat and cried until I was able to muster the courage to get myself up and go to the ICU.

As I sat in the chair in the corner of Juan's room in the Intensive Care Unit, I watched the doctors race to get him stabilized. I saw them take a blower heater and place it under the sheet that covered his little body in an effort to bring his body temperature back up to normal. They had to connect him to a ventilator because he could not breathe enough on his own to sustain his life. They began to insert needles into different areas of his body. I hurt so much for him. For the first time I could not kiss his booboo and make it feel better. I could not say anything to make him feel better. I had to stand back, watch and pray, somehow or someway he did not feel the trauma I knew he was going through.

His eyes remained closed, as though he did not want to see what was going on. Seeing that image reminded me of when I was a little girl and had to get a shot. I thought that if I closed my eyes it would not hurt as much. I imagined Juan closing his eyes, as I did, with hopes of not feeling the pain.

My prayers were interrupted when Cheryl, Juan's father's wife, entered his room. During the last conversation Cheryl and I had, she told me that she wanted nothing to do with my son. I often wondered how a woman who is a mother, could make such a cruel statement. I knew that with her telling me that she had to have a heart of stone. I vowed never to allow her to be alone with him because I believed in my heart that she would hurt him. I often prayed to God to give me the strength to forgive her. I had definitely accepted her feelings for my son, but her audacity to be in his room at this time was not acceptable to me. How dare she stand in his room as he lay there fighting for his life?

"Get her out of here!" I yelled. The doctors and nurses hurriedly pushed her into the hallway asking her to leave. When Juan's father, Anthony, entered the room, I could see the look of hurt on his face. We were not getting along prior my getting pregnant and after he walked away two months into my pregnancy, we were not exactly on speaking terms. To add insult to injury, he had gotten married when I was eight months pregnant.

For a moment, we seemed to be on the same page about Juan, but that lasted about as long as that statement. He started to blame me and call me names. I could feel the bitterness for Anthony begin to creep in, but I refused to allow it to make me lose my focus on my son. I walked to Juan's bedside and I began to pray.

As time passed, I would have to walk to and from the bathroom, passing through the waiting room, where Cheryl would be sitting. She looked at me with what seemed to be a smirk on her face. I could not understand how she expected me to accept her being at the hospital after she told me the way she felt about Juan. For some reason in my heart, I felt she wished the worst for him. My emotions took over and I stopped.

"Cheryl, you made it perfectly clear about the way you feel about Juan. He is in there fighting for his life! I want this time to be alone with my baby because I do not know if this is the last time we will have together. If you do not mind, I truly wish you would leave. I have to come through this area, and to see you here makes me sick to my stomach. Please give me this time with my son," I pleaded to her.

She responded, "I am not here for you and your baby, I am here for my husband."

Satan knows what buttons to push. Please know that I am not glorifying him, just acknowledging how if I was not careful he could easily take my focus off my son and he did. I walked around the corner only to remove my high heels and pantyhose and come back to the waiting room. My anger had gotten the best of me and I lost control. I began to hit her, dragging her off the couch on to the floor. My mother, sister and other family members rushed in and pulled me off of her.

"How can she even be here?" I yelled. "I am praying for my baby to live and she is praying for him to die!"

As she screamed for Anthony to come to her side, he rushed in. He saw the anger that her being there had caused, but he refused to ask her to leave. I cried for my son. How could I have allowed her to take my focus? As I went back to Juan's bedside, I asked God to help me look over her presence and to keep my attention on Juan.

The next several hours were very critical. The lead doctor was telling me that it was not looking good. He said Juan's right lung was beginning to develop air pockets and to harden. They needed to put a tube in to let the air out. I watched as they cut him without giving any sort of anesthetic to numb his pain. I prayed God would take the pain away from him.

The police investigator had arrived and waved his hand to get my attention because he wanted to ask me questions concerning my son's accident. I told him as much as I could with the information that had been given to me.

My cellular telephone rang constantly as the news about my son spread. Many of those who called were not sure of what to say. As the hours quickly passed and Juan's fight seemed to get harder, my fears were at an all time high. I looked to the doctors for some magic words or medicine that would make this all disappear and we could go home.

The next day brought forth more heartache. I placed a telephone call to my good friend Robin. As her telephone rang and rang, I opted not to leave a message, but instead to give her a call later. I learned of Robin's death after I received a call later that afternoon from another friend offering prayers for Juan and condolences for Robin.

I was hurting all over again. Robin had been diagnosed with Leukemia about a year before her death. She was on sick leave from her job. We would pray for her healing and she would always reassure me that she was going to beat the cancer that had so unexpectedly invaded her body. She told me that one day while eating lunch one of her teeth just fell out. It was through her dentist that she learned that she carried the horrible disease that robbed her of her young life. I knew that Robin would have been right here with me through all of this. I wept for her loss. I truly loved her and I knew she was one person I could count on for strength. I ached that she would not be able to help me through this.

I lay awake all night afraid that if I fell asleep I would open my eyes to more painful news. My staying up all night did me no good. The morning brought with it more shock and pain. I stood at my son's bedside with my eyes glued to the television set in total disbelief as I saw the World Trade Center crumble after terrorist flew two airplanes into it. What in the world was happening? Had the world come to an end and I was not informed?

The connection I felt to those in the World Trade Building and their families was strong. For, just like them, I did not see what was coming to me. I shared the pain of losing or almost losing someone you love dearly as the tragedy ripped my heart into pieces. I, too, felt the disillusion and the vacant disgust. I held on to Juan and I wept for those people, their families, and our country.

Later that day my cousin drove me home to pack some clothes and other personal items. As I unlocked my door, I hesitated because I knew everything was just as I had left it on Sunday morning. I scanned the den floor and saw Juan's toys lying around the room. My breaths began to shorten.

"You can do this," I told myself. I rushed down the hallway and more toys came into my view. I began to grab anything I could out of my drawers and stuffed them into my bag. I turned as I packed and pressed the message button on my telephone. I suddenly froze in place. The voice was Robin's.

"Hey Jackie, I was just calling to check on you. The police called me about the baby. Something happened and they cannot find you. I want to know if you are all right. Let me know if you need me, call me I will be around."

I began to literally choke. The combination of Juan's things and hearing Robin's voice was too much. I had to get out of my own home. I rushed outside to find relief. I got into the car.

"Are you okay?" my niece asked.

"I am okay. Drive me to Maria's house," I said. I had to see her. I had to hear her say she was sorry and to let her know that I forgave her. As I rang the bell my heart raced. Her husband came to the door and invited me in.

"Where is Maria?" I asked. Before he could answer, she came from down the hallway with tears in her eyes.

"I am so sorry, Jackie," she said. I held out my arms and embraced her.

"I forgive you," I said. Then I asked her to tell me what happened to Juan.

She explained, "I had mopped the kitchen floor and was going to mop the bathroom floor. I went to the bathroom and Juan was there behind me. I came back to the kitchen and he was in the play area playing with the toys. I went back to the bedroom and he was not there, but I did not think anything of it because he was playing with the toys. Delson came and knocked on my door and said, 'Mom I think Juan has drowned in the bucket of mop water.' At first I panicked, but then I started doing CPR on him and Monté called 911."

I could bear to hear no more. I told her that if she wanted to come to the hospital it was okay with me.

I got back to find that Juan was still fighting. I sat down next to my mother, laid my head on her shoulder, and wept. A few hours later a woman entered my son's room and asked if she could speak with me. We headed to the consultation room. She introduced herself and told me she was with the Department of Family and Children Services.

"It is formality, Ms. Boatwright, that we open a case concerning your child." This sickened me.

"Why are you investigating me? I caused no harm to my child. He was at his daycare," I insisted.

"Well, it is our policy to open the case on the parents when things like this happen," she said, placing a form in front of me. "I need for you to sign here saying that you will not allow Ms. Anderson to watch your children anymore."

To me that was one of those no-brainers. I had not done anything to my child, but here I was defending my character as a mother. I signed and was relieved it was over so I could go back and be with Juan.

I was saddened that due to Juan's illness I could not attend Robin's funeral. I still wanted to say good-bye to her. I had a friend drive me over to the funeral home where her body was. As I stood in the long line of people waiting to say their good-byes my mind reflected on the times we spent together. She was such a kind woman, always giving of herself. She put together my baby shower and brought food over when I came home from the hospital with Juan. She was a perfect example of a true missionary.

As I approached her casket, I smiled for she looked very pretty and her face presented such a peaceful smile. Not wanting to upset the tone of the room I rushed outside holding and sealing my tears. I loved her so much and was now feeling so many regrets, for it felt as though our time together was not long enough. I only hoped I said "I love you" enough to her.

I was walking out of the hospital one day when I ran into a young lady and her baby. He was in a wheel chair and had a trachea. I approached her as my heart went out for her and her baby. I asked her his name.

"Hey there, big guy," I said, gently stroking his forehead. He did not move.

"What happened to him?" I asked.

"He choked on a piece of popcorn and lost oxygen to his brain almost two years ago," she replied.

As I began to share with her Juan's story, I noticed she was wheelchair bound and had no legs. Her strength and her love for her son encouraged me that I could take care of Juan.

"The doctors wanted me to give up on my baby, but I refused. They thought because I have no legs that I would not be able to take care of him. But I proved them wrong," she said. We exchanged telephone numbers. We would call to check on each other's children.

As people visited Juan, they brought rumors of stories from the local paper. I had been hearing various comments from friends who had read in the paper, articles about Juan's accident. They told me about a story that Maria did not have a license. I needed to know if this was true. I remembered her showing me a license on my first visit to her center. In addition to this, I wanted to tell how I felt about Juan's accident.

I called the newspaper and asked for the name of the man who had written the articles. I told him that I would do the story on the condition that he gave God credit for my son surviving. I met Greg, the newspaper reporter in the hospital lobby. He looked so young and it crossed my mind that he may not have the experience to write a fair story. He assured me that he would write the story as to how I felt.

I shared with him my feelings, and what Maria told me had happened. I really, and truly, wanted every one to know that I was not angry and that I did not hate Maria for what happened to my son. All I wanted was to focus on Juan, my faith, with hopes that God would provide us with a miracle.

The lead doctor and his team of residents made their morning rounds. As the lead resident gave her report, I knew that some of it was not consistent with what I saw.

"I don't have a lot of faith in this team," I said, interrupting the report. I was hurting and everything that was coming out of her mouth was negative.

"Calm down, my baby," my mother said as she patted me gently on my back.

This statement obviously upset the lead doctor as he responded, "If you don't think this is a good team you can take him somewhere else."

My mother quickly subdued my anger.

"Baby, they are doing the best they can. Just pray." I walked out of the room.

As the days passed on, it seemed as though the doctors' interest in treating Juan begun to lessen. This angered me because I knew deep inside that it was about money. I was self-employed and without health insurance. I had been sent a bill for almost $6,000 within the first three days of Juan's hospital stay. What was I going to do with medical bills as excessive as Juan's had become? I knew I could not worry about money at that point. I had to keep my focus on was Juan.

The lead doctor called me into the consultation room. He told me, "Juan is brain dead and he is not going to ever recover or get any better than what you see now."

I thank God for giving me the strength to stand up for my baby. Once I saw that the doctors were giving up, I decided in my mind and in my heart that I was going to go with God. I had always prayed and believed and now I stood in a situation where those beliefs and prayers were all that I had to hold onto.

I told the doctor, "Thank you for your report, but I have decided to wait on another report from another doctor. You don't mind if I wait do you?"

He asked, "Who is this doctor?"

I looked him directly in his eyes and I said, "Dr. Jesus." He dropped his head as I walked out to return to Juan's room.

My decision to go with God reminded me daily that the war had just begun. I knew it was going to take every ounce of my strength and then some to stay on the battlefield.

Each doctor on Juan's team had a story to share with me about having to make the decision to remove a family member from life support. Well, it appeared that way anyway. They tried their best to convince me that pulling the plug on my son was the best thing to do. I often asked myself if they were asking me to pull the plug on him because there was truly no hope or was money the true reason they were trying so hard to convince me.

One doctor told me he had to pull the plug on his grandmother. "It was the best thing for us to do because of her condition," he said.

" I am sorry about your grandmother. How old was she?" I asked.

"She was ninety-one," he responded.

"I am sure she lived a good life, but my baby has just begun his life and I want him to live." I replied.

I was shocked at how my interpretation of hospitals was about saving lives and all the doctors that were treating Juan were asking me to end his life. I loved him so much and I refused not to give God an opportunity to help me.

One morning I became fed up with the blatant lack of interest in Juan's care.

I asked the lead doctor directly, "Is this about money?"

Of course, he denied that money was an issue.

"Ms Boatwright, we are going to treat Juan to the best of our ability," he said.

I reminded him of his oath as a doctor to care for my son regardless of our financial capabilities.

I told them, "You all need to relax, open you hearts and minds and allow my God to get in you so that he can heal Juan through you."

My faith level was so high, I do not think they understood me. Rumors had begun to circulate around the unit that I was in denial of Juan's condition. The more negativity I heard, the more I prayed. I would go to the chapel in the hospital and cry out to God to save Juan's life. Each night I sat up watching and hoping for a miracle from God, that God would show up and make them see that all I believed in was real.

As my faith grew so did my strength.

I remember sitting in the consultation room feeling broken and weary as Juan was once again in a code 99. My mind was racing in every different direction. My fears were trying desperately to overcome my faith. Also came negative thoughts of life insurance money, and being free of the responsibility of caring for a small child. Satan was trying to trap me. Realizing this was a great test of my faith, I immediately began to pray and rebuke Satan in the name of Jesus Christ.

"I want Juan!" I said.

Within a few minutes, I heard a knock on the door; it was the doctor telling me that Juan had stabilized. I thanked God for stepping in on time and for knowing my heart.

One night I told God, "Lord I want you to know that I trust you. I am going to sleep in the consultation room, you and your angels need to watch over Juan."

When I awoke, I found the nurses and doctors standing around Juan's bed and shaking their heads in total confusion. As I got closer to his room, I looked up at his monitor to see his little heart beating 258 beats per minute and climbing. Oh my God, I thought. As they walked out one by one, I knew that it was up to me to make the next move. I asked the nurse to lower his bed so I could lay down next to him and pray.

I held his head in my arms, and I began to pray.

"Lord, I know that you can help my baby. You are the same God today as you were when you took care of the Hebrew boys. The same God that protected Daniel in the lion's den, that raised Lazarus from the dead, made blind see, the lame walk and the dumb talk." I reflected on the message I had heard on September 9th at church. I began to repeat that day's text. "*It's your move.* God, *It's your move.*"

As I lay in the bed crying, and holding on to my baby, I noticed a nurse walk into my son's room and stumble backward with a startled look upon her face. Her face turned pale.

"What's wrong?" I asked as I sat up to look at the monitor. His heart rate had dropped to 158 beats per minute.

"Did you give him anything?" I asked.

She replied, "No."

I laid back down next to my son. I began to praise God for what I knew only he could have done. As I cried tears mixed with joy and sorrow, I heard a voice speak in the room.

"Hush!" The voice said. I looked around the room to find no one there but Juan and me. "I am going to heal that baby."

I knew it was the voice of God. I could feel the presence and a calm come over me.

I replied, "God, they say his lungs are severely damaged."

"I am going to fix his lungs," He said.

I asked, "What about his brain?"

"I am going to fix his brain," God replied.

"Lord, You see his heart is racing out of control."

"Hush, I am going to fix his heart. too."

Was I going crazy? No, I knew that the Holy Spirit had come to my rescue. I had to keep believing in Him, no matter what happened or how things looked.

The rest of the day brought forth a little more comfort, as Juan seem to settle down. As I walked down the hallway, my heart hurt, for it finally hit me that all the patients here were babies. The first room held a baby that had been there for about two or three years. His Mom and Dad visited him each day along with his two brothers. The nurses would often hold him and play with him because he had been there with them for a long time.

The second room held a baby who I would often see alone throughout the day. I would stand at his door and watch him play with the angels and coo into the air, waving his little hands as he seemed to focus on someone above him. He was born with heart problems.

Juan was in the center of the ICU. In the next room was a little girl battling cancer. Her mom told me her story. She would often come over and inquire about Juan. We would exchange inspirational books and pray for each other's child. She was a strong believer in God too, and her pastor would visit on a regular basis.

At the end of the hall was a little boy who also had heart problems. I prayed that God would heal all of these babies along with my Juan.

One night the baby that was alone most of the time went into a code 99. As the alarms sounded the nurses and doctors rushed to his room. His parents were unable to be reached. I stood there watching at Juan's door and praying that God keep him alive for his mother to be by his side.

God heard and answered my prayer. His mother came and the doctors told her his heart was failing. She sobbed as she went and kissed him good-bye. I wondered if she prayed to God to help him. As I walked toward her, her eyes said it all. If the eyes are truly the entrance to the soul, then hers showed the vast rip that she had just endured.

I asked her if she wanted to pray, she replied, "I am tired of him suffering. I want to let him go." He lay there until his little heart stopped.

For the hospital, this was common. They cleaned the room and prepared it for the next baby that would soon occupy it. The family of the baby with cancer moved into his room because it was larger. Another baby filled the room that they vacated.

A few mornings later as I lay asleep, I was awakened by the screams of a woman. "My baby! No God, my baby!"

I jumped up in fear, being I was asleep and caught off guard. I entered the waiting room to find the mother and father screeching in pain from the loss of their baby. Here again, as I watched in pain with them, I found myself holding on to the mother and crying with her for her child.

"Oh my God," I thought, "I am in the midst of death." I just kept praying harder and harder each day. In the midst of death, I must admit my fears started to set in. Was Juan next?

I began to recite the twenty-third Psalm. I knew that I must regain my faith in order to win this battle. I also knew that the Word of God gives us all so many days on this earth. I believed that our lives were already written prior to our arrival. Some have many days and others have only a short number of days. I prayed that Juan's life be written with many days. I had to remain focused on my faith. I knew that God can and will do. I needed the strength to wait on God even when there seemed to be no hope.

I refused to allow anyone to enter Juan's room with negative thoughts or conversation. Even when his body began to swell, distorting his face, I held on to my faith and I told him how beautiful he was.

I had received a telephone call that the lead investigator wanted me to come to the police station. I went there and they told me that they wanted to press criminal charges against Maria for what happened to Juan.

"Please don't send her to jail. I don't think she meant to hurt my child," I pleaded with the investigator.

"This is not your call, Ms. Boatwright, it's ours. We plan to recreate the crime scene to find out what really happened," he said.

Another gentleman, from the DA's office, entered the room. He began to explain the type of sentence given, for what they wanted to charge Maria with.

"Please, I don't want Maria to go to jail," I pleaded again.

The investigator asked if he could show me the type of bucket the water was in that she used to mop the floor.

My throat immediately got full as I softly whispered, "He was bigger than that bucket, he could have turned it over."

"We feel the same way, Ms Boatwright, this is why we want to find out if the way they are telling us it happened is really the way it happened," the man from the DA's office said.

The investigator could see the look on my face and said, "I see how much this means to you, so I am going to drop it for that reason." I thanked him and left.

After leaving the police station, my thoughts were going back and forth about what happened on September 9th. I knew that I had to let it go. I was just so glad that Juan was alive and I did not want to focus how or why this happened to him. I must admit after seeing the bucket, I found myself praying diligently to make it through my doubts, as they so often would creep in.

One day, as I sat watching television I looked up to find a woman was standing at the door to Juan's room. I could see her mouth moving, but I could not hear her because of her soft-spoken voice.

As I walked to her, she asked, "What is wrong with your baby?"

I told her Juan's story. "Why are you so sad?" I asked."

"My baby is in the room on the end and he is not doing good."

I told her, "You must trust in God."

"Will you pray for him?" she asked.

"Sure," I replied. As I put on the gown and gloves to enter his room, I silently asked God to be with me. "He is so handsome," I said to her. I told her, "Now that you have prayed to God, act as though your blessing had come." We would go on to find comfort in each other through our conversations. She would often share with me her dreams of my baby and her baby waking up at the same time. What a beautiful dream!

The next morning I received a call from the social worker asking me to come to the business office to sign for payment of the hospital bill. As I rode the elevator down to the first floor, I could not help but notice the eerie feeling that had come upon me earlier that morning. I was not sure of what it meant I just knew that I did not like it.

I kept saying to myself, " I must go to the chapel and pray." I felt that if I could just pray God would relieve me of what ever it was I was about to encounter. After leaving the business office, I went around the corner to the chapel and I prayed to God asking him to remove whatever negative there was about this feeling.

"God please give me some reassurance that Juan is going to be okay," I prayed.

As I rode the elevator back up to the ICU, I felt somewhat better but not totally relieved of this feeling.

I walked into Juan's room and there was a woman standing next to my mother. Fearing the worst, I asked, "Mom, what has happened?"

"Everything is okay with the baby. This woman is here to see you," my mother replied.

As she came around to the side of Juan's bed where I stood and said, "I know that you don't know me because I don't know you. God woke me up in my sleep last night and told me I had to come tell you, your baby has already been healed. But you have to let go of any anger you have."

I assured her that I forgave Maria days ago. I looked at her in awe because I knew that I was downstairs praying to God for reassurance of Juan being okay and this woman was standing here with an answer to my prayer. "Who did you come to visit?" I asked.

"You are the only reason I am at this hospital. I traveled more than fifty miles to come here to tell you this," she answered.

We began to praise God together. We exchanged telephone numbers and she left. Later that night I called her and she went on to tell me how she found us.

She explained, "I don't get the Augusta newspaper, but my mother-in-law does. She was on vacation and asked me to get her mail and to toss the newspaper because by the time she returned home, it would be old news anyway. I had been throwing them all away when I decided to read the one that had the story on your baby. I felt bad about him and prayed for him. I thought that was all I had to do. Later that same night, as I tried to sleep. I was literally tossed in my bed. The voice of God told me that I had to get up and go tell you that the baby has been healed. I was unsure about all of this. The next morning, it was on my heart, that I had to come there to tell you that your baby has been healed. My two daughters and I got in the car and headed for our appointment, I passed the road that I needed to turn on. My daughters questioned me. I told them that I had to go tell this woman that her baby is healed. I asked God that if this is what he wanted me to do to please give me some sort of sign. Immediately a song came on the radio about being obedient to God. I knew then that I had to go. Every traffic light that I got to was on green."

I praised God for the timing and for sending this message of confirmation to me.

A few days later I stood at the desk next to Juan's bed as I talked on the telephone. "Oh my God, he moved his hand!" I said to the nurse.

Her response was one of total disbelief. "That is just a reflex, and I didn't see him move."

As I started to argue with her, Juan raised his little hand again and he made a fist. "There, he did it again!" I screeched.

"Umm," she replied.

"I am not crazy. I know I saw him move!"

Another nurse overhearing the conversation had walked into the room. "You are not crazy, Ms. Boatwright. I saw him move, too."

I embraced her and shed tears of joy as I thanked her. Juan also had started to take breaths on his own. Because of his breathing over the ventilator, the nurse told me doctors had decided to remove his tube to see if he could breathe enough on his own to keep him alive without the ventilator. I waited patiently for the doctor to come.

His arrival was more painful than I had expected. When he walked into the room, he grabbed a chair, propped his feet up, placed both hands behind his head, "If he doesn't breathe enough on his own, do you want us to let him die?"

I could have punched him. How could he even ask me such a question? "No, you do not let him die! You insert that tube back in him and you let him breathe again!"

Seeing he had upset me, he tried to explain, "We just have to give you all of your options, Ms Boatwright."

"You listen to me, Juan dying is not an option!"

He left knowing that I was angry at the way he approached me. As the moment came for the trial of his breathing on his own, my heart raced wide open as though I were in the Indianapolis 500. Clinging to my friend's hand, the tube was removed.

As his oxygen level dropped, the rush to get the tube reinserted began. I crumpled to the floor, briefly losing conscience. As my sight came back, I was surrounded by nurses.

"Oh, my God!" I cried.

"He is okay," a voice in the crowd said.

Another voice asked, "Do you want me to get the chaplain?"

"Yes," I whispered.

As I was being helped to a nearby chair the chaplain came and knelt next to me. I was desperately hoping that we would pray and he would remind me of the power of God.

"I am so sorry things aren't going the way you want them to," he said.

As I sat there waiting for more, I realized that was it. He had said all he was going to say to me.

"Everybody just leave!" I said, as I got up and walked to Juan's bedside. "Okay my baby, we are rushing God, he is not ready yet, so we are going to get back on our bandwagon of faith and we are going to wait on him." I began to praise God as I wiped the tears from my face.

I could not understand why a minister of all people would make no attempt to reassure my faith in God. I remember this one minister calling me on the phone.

He said, "I am going to pray, but remember sometimes even when we pray, things go the other way."

My stomached tightened as I refused to believe that God would confuse me. Why would His word say that it would be granted if I trusted in Him with all my heart and then He not do it?

Just so you know, He is not a God of confusion. His word says that anything we ask in the name of Jesus, it will be given. He does not second guess the things that He says He will give to us.

My heart was led to change the way I prayed. I was always taught to say, "Lord if it is your will, do this or do that."

He says He will do what he tells us in the Bible. By adding that phrase leaves room for doubt or lack of faith. So that when our blessings don't happen we can say that it was not God's will. Or was it truly our lack of faith that was the reason of our not receiving the promises of God?

The word says that "Lord if it is your will" should be applied to things that we say we are going to do, for example, to go here or to do this. Because we can only do what He allows us to do. But everything He says He will do will be done; according to your faith in Him.

The morning would bring new hopes and leave old hopes behind us. Another trip home to get clean clothing and check my mail encouraged my new hopes. I was shocked to see the amount of my cellular telephone bill.

"Oh, my God, I need this phone. Lord, this is the only way the hospital can contact me when I step outside those doors," I prayed.

I picked up my home telephone and called the cellular company to set up payment arrangements.

"How may I help you?" the voice said. I explained to her all that had happened and the reason why my bill was so much.

"Can you verify the last four numbers of your social security number?" she asked. I told her the digits.

"I am sorry Ms. Boatwright, your cellular phone has been disconnected for non-payment and due the amount of the bill we are unable to turn it back on until we receive payment," she said.

At that moment, my cellular telephone lying on the table rang.

"Could you please hold for me for a second?" I asked. I answered my cell telephone. It was the hospital wanting to know the time of my return, because I needed to sign some documents.

"I'll be back in about an half hour." I said and hung up.

As I returned to the line with the cell telephone representative, I asked again, "Are you sure my telephone is disconnected?"

She angrily repeated all of my account information. "Not only is it disconnected, it has been for two weeks and as I told you before, we are not going to turn it back on until we get some money!"

I redialed the hospital's number and I was shocked when I heard, "MCG, how may I help you?"

I thanked the woman at the telephone company for her time. God had again answered my prayers. I returned to the hospital.

As the day turned to night, I kissed Juan on his forehead, "Night, night my sweet baby." I walked over to the cot where Dereck was asleep and kissed him as well.

I sat down and removed my shoes. As I began to lay my body down, a voice, which I will call from this point on, the Holy Spirit, said to me, "Get up, Jackie. Get up and go to Juan's bed."

I raced in a pace as hurriedly as the tone of the voice.

The voice said, "Rub his foot and watch it move."

I rubbed Juan's foot and as the voice said, it moved. I backed away from the bed in fear of what was happening.

"God, if this is you, you need to let me know because I think that I am losing my mind," I said in a low tone voice being careful not to have anyone hear me talking to myself.

I walked back to the cot and attempted to lie down again.

"Get up, Jackie. Get up you are going to miss it! Get up! Get up!"

Again, I rushed to the sound of the voice of the Holy Spirit, to Juan's bed.

"Rub his foot and watch it move," he said.

I rubbed his foot and the foot moved. I began to cry.

"How are you going to tell it, Jackie?" He asked.

"What do you mean?" I said.

"How are you going to tell everybody about all of this?" He asked.

"I don't know Lord, but I am going to make them know that it is you." I replied.

He then said, "I am going to prove to you I am who I am. A nurse is going to come into the room. I am going to have her leave by making the alarms in the next room go off."

As I lay there with my head under the covers, I heard the nurse enter the room. She acknowledged herself by speaking to me. My son's alarm immediately went off and quickly silenced. Just as I thought that it was not going to happen, I hear all of the alarms in the next room go off. The nurse raced out of the room.

"I told you," He said. What was happening to me?

As the hours rolled by, Juan was still holding on and I can tell you each day got easier and easier. My Pastor and church family, as well as my friends and family, would visit from day to day. One or another of them would break down in tears upon looking at Juan's swollen, tube filled body. I comforted them assuring them that he was going to be okay. They could not understand why I was not torn apart with all of this.

We walked the floor praying for the other babies and their families. More and more, I begun to understand my mission.

As my eyes opened to Sunday morning, I heard the voice of God speak to me again.

"Get up and go home and put on the same clothes you wore on the day this happened, I am going to send you to a church," He said.

I immediately got up and went home to get dressed. I did as God asked and put on the same clothing. As I drove down the street not sure of which church I would attend, my mind thought of several churches that I had attended or that I knew of. Each thought brought forth the same answer from the voice of God.

"That is not the one," He would reply.

"Lord I know that you are not going to have me go back to South Carolina to church?" I asked.

"No," He replied. "I am going to tell you where to go."

"Wherever you send me let me get something out of the service as well as give something back." I prayed.

As I drove around the city, I even pulled into a church parking lot the voice of God said. "This is not the one."

Along my journey, the car began to pull to the right. It was almost as if I could not control it. I did not fight as I steered into the church parking lot. As I stared at the marquee, it read Methodist.

I quickly questioned God. "God, are you sure this is the right one for I am Baptist?"

"This is the one," He said.

I got out of the car and stood in confusion as to which set of double doors I was to enter. I glanced back at the marquee to check the time of the service. As I turned back around, one of the double doors had partially opened.

I walked up the stairs and went inside I sat down in the sanctuary, my attention was focused on the children's Sunday School class. Their lesson was about when God raised Lazarus from the dead.

As the class ended and the teachers asked for questions and comments, I stood and told them about Juan. The two women in the class had read about Juan in the newspaper and asked me to come up to the area where the class was. The man, whom I later found out was the associate pastor, asked me how I found out about their church. I immediately started telling him of the voice of God and what God had said for me to do.

As I conversed with the women concerning Juan, another man entered the room. He was the Pastor of the Church. I shared with him how I came to their church. After a brief conversation, he asked me to speak to his congregation during the morning worship service. I was totally shocked. I had not prepared a speech. I agreed.

As I told Juan's story, there was hardly a dry eye in the place. I left and returned to the hospital with a new message in my heart and mind. *Obedience is Better Than Sacrifice.* The minister had delivered a soul-stirring message about how God had asked Abraham to sacrifice his son Isaac and how Abraham's obedience led to God's sparing Isaac's life.

I drifted off to sleep with unspeakable joy in my heart. I awakened, and saw a good friend of mine standing at Juan's bedside.

"Miss Debbie, why didn't you wake me up?" I said to her.

"I knew you were tired and I thought that I would let you sleep," she replied.

I met Miss Debbie, a second grade teacher, through her membership at my fitness club. She and I had become close friends. We shared many spirit-filled conversations as we walked the treadmill. Whenever someone asked me to pray with them, I immediately grabbed her by the arm because I knew she was very close to God.

"So, how have you been doing?" she asked.

"I am fine," I responded.

She always brought me some sort of gift. Her compassion and sincere love for my children and me always touched my heart.

"Jackie, there is this family on the fourth floor that I would like for you to pray with."

She went on tell me that the young man was in a three-wheeler accident where he had a head injury that left him fighting for his life. She said that they were not expecting him to live.

"Let's go!" I said.

"You do not have to go now, I know you are tired," Miss Debbie said. I assured her it was okay and we headed to the fourth floor.

When we arrived, the family was crying and broken. The mother and father sat huddled together in the hallway. As the mother clutched her Bible and sobbed, my heart went out to her. I knelt down in front of them and I told them the story of Abraham and Isaac. I told them that God did not want their son. He wanted them. I prayed with them and shared in their pain and heartache.

Miss Debbie and I returned to Juan's floor where we said goodbye at the elevator. Just before she left she handed me a stack of letters from her second grade class. They had begun to write me the most heartfelt letters encouraging me to continue praying and believing that Juan was going to be okay.

I could have held on to her forever as she embraced me and said, "I love you."

As I kissed Juan softly on his cheek, I took a deep breath to savor his sweet smell. I loved him so much. As night began to fall and my eyes got heavy, I said a prayer to God and drifted off to sleep.

The next morning I awoke to find Juan still holding on, my heart was filled with new hopes for his healing.

As the nurses and hospital staff walked in and attended to Juan, I would casually ask, "Do you believe in God?" Some of them said, yes they did believe in God.

One therapist told me he did not believe, "If there is a God; why does he let all these things happen to babies?" he said.

While he examined my son's breathing machine, I immediately asked God to forgive him and to anoint his hands as he worked with Juan.

Later that afternoon God spoke to me again.

"Go back to the fourth floor." I went back to find the family of the young man even more broken then before. As I stood there, I silently asked God for the right words to say to them. The young man's wife was truly taking the doctor's latest news very hard. I asked her to come into the hallway. My intentions were to give her my shoulder to cry on and to tell her to be strong that he was going to be okay.

As I embraced her, I asked, "Do you know who God is?"

She replied, "No."

"Well, let me tell you who He is!" I said to her. "He is big and bad enough to do anything He wants, and that includes heal your husband."

As we walked to the staircase and sat down, I asked her, "Do you want to be saved?"

With a look of confusion, she did not respond. I told her that her salvation and devotion to God would help bring forth the healing for her husband.

According to the Bible, I said, "All you have to do is to confess your sins and believe that Jesus was raised from the dead and you will be saved."

She immediately repeated the scripture of salvation and we embraced with unspeakable joy at her being saved. I told her that her salvation was a daily task that she would have to work at to live the life God has intended for her.

I am so glad that God gave me understanding to know, according to the word, all He requests is your mere acknowledgment of your sins and of Jesus' living. With this acknowledgement, you will know that you can call upon him and He will come to your side at any given moment.

I was amazed this young woman did not know that God was waiting to help her, all she had to do was, call on Him. We walked back into the waiting room with the rest of her family and shared the good news.

I was truly overjoyed as I walked back to Juan's room praising God for what he had just used me to do. I kept telling myself that I am not worthy of such a great task, but my heart told me that God saw something in me I did not see in myself.

The next morning the social worker approached me about going to the social security office to apply for disability for Juan. As my faith had strengthened, I told the man that Juan was not disabled and I did not want to apply for disability. He looked at me strangely and said that he admired my faith, as he walked out of the room.

I gained this awesome amount of strength that kept on coming and at times I amazed myself with all that I had begun to handle. There were times when things were so bad with Juan. I asked myself, why I was not crying. I would often attempt to cry and found that I was unable to do so. No tears would fall, instead my heart felt happy and content. For the first time in my life, I truly understood the passage in the Bible that says God will give you strength that surpasses all understanding.

Later that night my pastor and his wife came to visit Juan. I could see the look of fear in his face. I told him of my faith in God and what I knew that God was going to do for Juan. As we prayed for Juan, I prayed for my pastor's strength.

The next day the young man on the fourth floor and his family were on my heart and mind.

When I got to the waiting room, the young man's mother asked me, "Who keeps calling you to come here? You seem to come when we need you."

I began to share with her the voice of God telling me to come. We prayed and I left. Later that night, as I slept, sharp pain in my stomach awakened me. I sat up hoping it would go away. The pain did no stop. I walked half asleep to the bathroom and I reached to open the door.

The voice of God said, "You have to go back to the fourth floor."

"But God, it's almost two o'clock!"

He said, "I know, but you have go back, go put your shoes on."

I walked back to Juan's room, sat down on the cot, and began to put on my shoes. I picked up my Bible and asked myself what was I going to say to this family.

God said, "Close the book. I will tell you what to say when you get there." I walked down the long corridor and got on the elevator that led to the fourth floor.

As I stood outside in the fourth floor corridor, I saw the young man's mother and father as they flipped out a blanket preparing to lie down and rest. As my eyes scanned the room, I saw that they were the only two people awake. I wondered to myself why I was here.

The father looked up and saw me standing there, he rushed out, grabbed my hands, and asked me to tell him what to do because they were saying that his son was not going to make it.

"All I know to tell you is keep praying and trusting in God." I said.

"No, you pray!" he responded, as he grabbed me by the hand leading me to his son's bedside.

This was the first time that I had actually seen the young man. I could hardly swallow as I looked at his comatose body, filled with tubes and simply laying there, just as Juan laid in his bed. I walked to his bedside, reached back and held his mother's hand as she joined hands with her husband.

I laid my hand on his shoulder and said aloud, "God, I don't know why I am here, but You asked me to come so have Your way."

I immediately began to weep, but I was aware that the weeping was not my own. All of a sudden, my body began to shiver from the top of my head to the bottom of my feet. As I prayed to God, I started speaking in other tongues and languages. I was frightened but realized that my body was a being used as a vessel by God. I stood in fear and allowed the Holy Spirit to continue.

The father and mother were afraid. The father ran from the room. The mother could only get the distance of my arm.

I heard the father ask her, "My God what is wrong with her?"

She replied, "I don't know, but I think she is talking with God."

Finally, it was over. I felt weak and drained as we walked back into the waiting area.

As I stood there in tears praising God, I looked to find the mother and father on their knees in front of me asking, "Tell us what we need to do to be saved."

I replied, "Romans 10:9."

They began to flip through their Bibles to find the scripture, I asked that they close the book and repeat after me. They did and were saved that very moment.

As I walked back down the long corridor leading to Juan's room at ICU, I talked with God.

"Please make this miracle happen. These people were saved according to my faith."

As I reached the door that led to the ICU, I looked into the glass window in front of me that overlooked the parking lot. Because of the lighting, the glass gave a reflection of the long corridor that was behind me. I saw an image walking behind me and as soon as I saw it, it disappeared into thin air. My fears heightened as I rang the buzzer repeatedly to enter the ICU area. When I finally got back into bed, I lay there unable to sleep. I wondered what all that had happened to me meant. Would people believe me when I told them?

The next morning I called Maria to ask about her insurance carrier. I was totally shocked to find out that she was not insured. I immediately called the Department of Human Resources to ask if they were aware that she had no liability insurance on the day care business.

"We don't require day care centers that we license to have insurance," the lady on the other end of the telephone said to me.

"You have to be kidding, right? That is totally ridiculous!" I said slamming the telephone down on the receiver.

As I thumbed through the yellow pages to find an attorney, my attention stopped on the second name that I saw. I dialed the number and asked to speak with an attorney. I briefly explained to him my situation. He agreed to come the next day to the hospital to meet me.

Sitting down in the chair, I dialed Maria's number again to get the name of her homeowner's insurance.

"It is not in my name it is in my husband's name," she said.

"It doesn't matter whose name it is in, I just need to know the name of the carrier so that I can try to get some help with Juan's medical bills," I said to her.

"I will ask my husband who it is because I don't know," she responded.

"Okay," I said and hung the telephone up.

She does not have insurance. How could this be? Oh my God, I thought! What am I going to do?

The next day as I sat in the waiting room awaiting the arrival of the attorney, I prayed that this would all somehow work itself out. I looked to find a tall, young gentleman coming toward me. He extended his hand and introduced himself.

"My name is Richard Ingram. I am the attorney you spoke with on the phone on yesterday."

"Thank you so much for coming," I said, firmly shaking his hand.

"You know, God has to be in this. I have already tried and won a case just like this," he said.

When he spoke of God sending him, my heart was overjoyed with the fact that he knew God. I felt my prayer was answered. He went on to tell me that he would try to find out the name of the homeowner's insurance company.

I asked him if he would like to see my baby. He said yes and we walked into Juan's room. I could see the compassion in his eyes as he looked around the room and at Juan.

"I am going to do all I can to help you with this," he said, as he left.

The next few days brought good news - Juan was stable enough to go home!

The doctors told me that I would have to prove that I could take care of him, before I would be allowed to take him home. Just the thought of going home was music to my ears. I believed in my heart that if I took Juan home he would get better. I became like a sponge soaking in every bit of knowledge about his care. I had been the type of person who had a weak stomach, but my love for Juan cured that.

As time progressed and Juan got a little better, we moved out of ICU to the fourth floor. The fourth floor is the next step before going home. Each day brought forth more excitement about the possibility of going home. We had spent over 30 days in the ICU and I was ready to go home. I could not believe that it was almost November. The thought of spending Thanksgiving at home was a pleasant one. The feel of my bed and not living out of a suitcase brought joy as well. The transition to the fourth floor went smoothly.

The nurses told me that I had to have a back up caregiver trained to take care of Juan. My mind raced with thoughts of who would I ask to take on such great task. I immediately thought of a close friend of mine. She had always been a good friend to me. She was even there for Juan's birth and was christened as his Godmother. She worked as certified nurses' assistant in a neighboring hospital. Almost everyday on her way home from work she would stop in and visit Juan. Even if I had stepped away from his room briefly, I knew that she had been there because of the set of red lips on Juan's cheek where she would plant her kisses. We had met sometime ago and become close friends as we shared in each other's joys and sorrows.

I called her at her job to ask her to be my backup caregiver.

"Hi, girl. This is Jackie. I called to ask a favor of you. The hospital is going to let me take my baby home but I need a backup person that can help me take care of him to get the state to provide him home nursing care," I told her.

"What would I have to do?" she asked.

"Well they told me that they would spend the next few weeks training me and my backup caregiver on how to take care of him. Once we demonstrated that we could do the procedures then I could take him home," I responded.

"Let me talk to my husband about it and see what he thinks," she said.

"Okay. I will talk with you tomorrow," I said.

I did not have any reason to suspect that he would tell her she could not help me, because he was also christened as Juan's Godfather.

Weeks went by and I did not hear from her. My fears set in and I broke down. I was afraid that they were not going to let me bring him home. I called my mother.

"Hi, mom."

"What's wrong my baby? Is Juan okay?"

"Yes, he is doing fine," I said. "They told me that I could take him home if I had someone else trained to take care of him."

"That's good," she responded.

"I asked my friend, but I have not heard back from her," I said. "Mom, all I want to do is to get him home. I will give up everything to take care of him and to try to get him back up on his feet. Will you please come up here and help me."

"Sure baby, you know I will do all I can to help you. Mama is old now, but I will do all that I can."

"Thank you, mama," I said tearfully.

A few days later, my friend stopped by and asked if Dereck could go home to spend the night with her son. I let him go. I noticed that she still did not mention anything about what I had asked her to do in regard to Juan's going home.

The next morning when she dropped Dereck off at the hospital on her way to work she said. "I asked my husband about what you asked us to do and he said 'No, No, No, child!' What if something happened, you would blame us."

My heart was so sad for her to think that I would blame them for anything happening to Juan.

"First of all, my mom has agreed to be my secondary caregiver," I said. "Secondly, I am not taking my baby home to die. I am taking him home to live. If God chose to take him, then why would I blame you? Tell me this. You stood before God, my pastor and my family saying that you would take on the responsibility of being Godparents to my son. What if something had happened to me, what would happen to Juan?"

"We would take him," she said shyly looking away.

"You can't convince me of that. You don't want to help me with him I know that you would not take him on your own in his condition."

I think we both knew that the special bond that we once shared had just been severed. Would we ever be the way we were?

I knew I had to stay focused on Juan, he was my baby, and as his mother, no matter who walked out on him, I was not going to give up on him. I loved him and if it meant losing those I thought were my friends, then that was a price I would have to pay to help him get well.

The room we occupied on the fourth floor was much roomier than the one at ICU. It resembled more like a hotel suite. My mom, Dereck and I settled in easily. We had become more relaxed and often found ourselves laughing and cracking jokes. Hamburgers and French fries had been our supper for quite some time, but none of us complained about it.

It was refreshing to finally be around so many God-fearing nurses and assistants. So many of them joined hands with me and prayed for Juan. They shared in my hopes for a miracle. I returned to Juan's room one afternoon, to find my Bible open to the fifth chapter in the book of James. My eyes focused immediately on the words.

It said, "Is any sick among you? Let him call for the elders of the church; and let them pray over him, anointing him with oil in the name of the Lord: and the prayer of faith shall save the sick, and the Lord shall raise him up."

I ran out of the hospital and went to the grocery store. I bought some oil so that I could do as the verse said about anointing his head with oil. I had to trust God because he had brought me to the point of where I now stood.

We had so much to learn and in such a short time. The information at times was confusing due to the medical terms the nurses used during our training. I would often watch in disgust at the look upon my mother's face. I had learned to master the terms quickly, but my seventy-five year old mother was totally lost. Her not understanding stood out as she attempted to demonstrate the techniques. This made me so angry.

One day I snapped. "You all just stop! This is too much too soon!" I said running from the room.

I went into the waiting area, sat in a chair and let my emotions go. I began to blame myself for Juan's accident, and for having to put my mother through this. After about 30 minutes had passed and my self-anger was subdued, I walked back into the room.

"Listen, you are talking over my mother's head. When we get home, we are not going to be talking like this. Put this in terms that she will know exactly what you are saying. Use visual descriptions. Just say it like you know we would say it."

I think they finally understood my frustration. One of them wrote across the chalkboard in Juan's room, *"Use layman's terms when training."*

With our new teaching method, my mother became the Florence Nightingale of the fourth floor. As our going home was quickly approaching, the social worker gave me the name of the nursing company that would assisting me with Juan's home care.

"They will be contacting you soon and coming to meet you," she said handing me their business card. I placed the card on the table after looking at it. The next day, I shared with two nurses' assistants that Juan would be going home soon. I went on to tell them about the nursing company.

"Oh, my goodness," the female assistant said under her breath.

"What do you mean?" I asked.

"I have used that company for quite sometime. I am a mother of a vent-dependant child. They hardly ever show up and they overmedicated my son," she said.

The overmedicating scared me. I called the social worker and shared with her the information I received from the nursing assistant.

"Can you give me the name of another company?" I asked.

"I am sorry, Ms. Boatwright, they are the only company that cares for children on home ventilators," she responded. She went on to say, "I know the manager and I will speak with her about your concerns and have her come talk with you before you leave the hospital." I felt a little better.

The next morning, the manager of the nursing company came to visit me. She introduced herself and asked if she could have a moment to speak with me. We walked into the waiting area and sat in the two chairs that overlooked the parking lot. My nerves were on full alert as my heartbeat began to speed up. I took a deep breath and listened carefully as she shared her company's history.

"I know that you have heard some horrible things about our company but those things happened a long time ago. Since I have been manager, things have changed for the better. I promise you, Ms. Boatwright, nothing like that would ever happen to your child if you trust us to take care of him."

Her girl next door look and sweet tone reassured me to trust them to take care of him. My nerves must have been reassured as well, for the beat of my heart had slowed by the end of our conversation.

The next few days were the count down to November 13, our release day. I was running back and forth between the house and the hospital, trying to get things prepared for Juan to come home. I decided to exchange his room with the room that Dereck slept in. As I moved his crib from the back bedroom to the bedroom up the hall, my mind reflected. Juan had only slept in this crib overnight once. That was the night before his accident.

I had bought a new Bible and given my old Bible to Dereck. I had taken Juan and placed him in the crib. I sat back on the bed and began to read my Bible.

"Go to sleep, Juan," I had said to him.

He did not like that crib. But the funny thing about him was whenever you said to him, "Night, night," he would lie down no matter what the time of day it was. I had often laughed at how he comprehended that phrase.

Juan had been standing in the crib crying to get out. When I had said to him, "Night, night," he had laid down. He did not stop crying, but he did lie down. That had gone on until he fell asleep. I had awoke the next morning telling him how big of a boy he was for sleeping in his bed. Juan had normally slept with me and I had missed him being there throughout the night.

The crib caught the doorway, and my struggle to get it loose brought me back to reality. I began to cry. I sat on the floor all alone crying aloud and painfully about Juan and the turn my life had taken. I laid curled in a fetal position begging God to hold me. As I sobbed, I felt a peace within myself and a gentle rocking of my body that held me until my crying stopped. I got up, finished Juan's room and later returned to the hospital.

Juan had grown so much in such short time. He literally grew before my eyes. None of his T-shirts fit anymore. My baby was growing and I could not see him reach the milestones, the way a mother would want to.

The day before Juan's release, the nurses from the company came to meet us at the hospital. The manager introduced them as her best nurses.

"This is Tammy and Alice. They both have been with our company for a long time and are two of the best nurses we have. This is Bethany. She is in training. Tammy has a lot of experience with home transport and will be the one riding with you to watch over Juan on the trip home." We shook hands and greeted each other with a smile.

"Okay, I am just ready to go home," I said.

She went on to explain the roles of the other two nurses in our trip home. Shortly thereafter, they left.

I could hardly sleep thinking about the next day. We were going home!

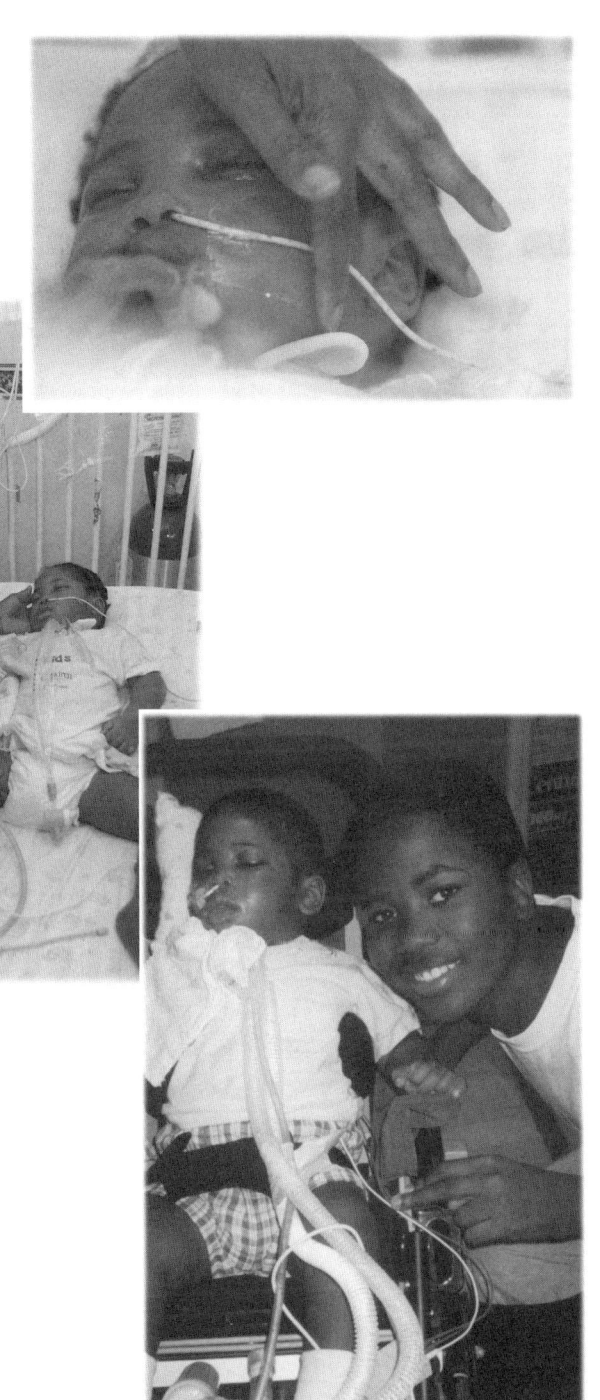

Photos courtesy of
Andrew Davis Tucker
The Augusta Chronicle

Chapter 2

After spending sixty-five days in the hospital, we arrived home without incident and settled Juan in his room. I was elated to be able to take my shoes off and just to relax on my own bed. Juan was to have 24 hour nurses care for his first two weeks at home. As our first night home settled in, the nurse woke me up.

"Ms Boatwright, Juan's oxygen saturation is dropping and I don't know how to give him oxygen in line to help him maintain his levels," she said.

I jumped up and rushed in the room to assist her. I began using the ambu-bag to give him oxygen. I instructed her to call 911.

I could see the level of panic on her face as she screamed. "His trachea is plugged!"

I told her, to calm down and that we would change the trachea. I quickly removed the trachea and replaced it with a new one. Juan still needed to receive oxygen.

The company that set up his ventilator failed to instruct us on how to put oxygen in line for Juan to receive. I told her to bag him, as I searched for the number of the nurse from the previous shift. She had told me before she left that she would be staying the night down the street from my home at her father's house.

I found the number and called. I told her what was going on with the oxygen. She said she was on her way. The ambulance arrived within minutes. We realized that as long as we bagged Juan, he was not in distress, but we needed to get him some oxygen.

As the previous nurse arrived, she rigged up the O2 line so that he could get the oxygen. It was not connected the way it should have been, but it was working and that was all that mattered.

After the paramedics and everyone left. I sat down in the chair and took a deep breath. My moment of relief was interrupted when the nurse burst out in tears.

"What's wrong?" I asked.

She sobbed saying, "I'm sorry."

"For what? He is fine," I said.

I consoled her until she was able to regain herself. My mother stood at the door looking confused as to why I was the one doing the consoling.

The next few days seemed to go well. There were no major problems with Juan and I was finally able to relax a little.

I sat in the chair in Juan's room reading letters from Miss Debbie's second grade class. I often thought of the many adults that didn't know what to say to me about Juan's situation and these children gave me so much strength and hope.

I want to share with you a few of their letters just as they wrote them. I will write this in their grammar and using their spelling. They are 7-8 year olds.

This particular letter is from a little girl named Whitney. *"This is for Juan, Please come back for Jackie. She really misses you very much and I also misses you too. I love you a lot please love me to because I have not stop prying about you. I promise I will not forget about you. Love Whitney"*

The next letter read, *"We hope you fill better. You are the best mom I had seened. I still pray for you at night. Jacob"*

I cried for this child could see that I was indeed trying to be a good mother to Juan and in his little eyes I was the best.

I read on, *"Dear Ms. Jackie how is Juan I hope hi is doing okay in that hospital but this is the only thing you need to remember that God is healing him as hard as he can. And God not going to give up on him as long as you keep praying. But most of all thing abot how Juan loves you and you love him. Your frind Dallas.*

The last one that I will share come from Shiamante, *"Dear Juan, I love you so much. I hope you get well soon! Remember God is with all of his children, don't for get I am pray for you. And I will allway rember you."*

I cried as I read the hearts of these children. I could feel how hard they tried to make me and Juan feel better.

As the Thanksgiving holiday neared, my joy level escalated. I knew that we would not be able to visit our family, but just knowing that we would be home for Thanksgiving made my heart feel glad.

Each day brought with it something new. I was amazed at the level of understanding that God had given me with taking care of Juan. I still look at all that I did with wonder, because I knew my level of tolerance when it came to very sick people. I had none. My stomach would always be in knots by the sight of blood, and yet here I was doing it all and not having any problems dealing with it. All that my heart knew and felt was Juan.

I spent many nights sleeping on the floor or in the chair in his room. It was very hard for me to deal with leaving him alone for quite sometime. I must admit that I blamed myself a lot of times for leaving him the day of his accident. I would find myself standing at his bed making promises not to ever leave him alone. It was even hard to go to the grocery store or to do other things outside of the house. Each time I tried my fears would send me rushing to get home to him. Being into the word I knew that God did not give us the spirit of fear. I kept telling myself this until I was able to be away from him without having an anxiety attack worrying about him.

Although I knew Juan was in a coma, it looked as though he was only sleeping, and with the most peaceful look on his face. I believed in my heart that he was not suffering. As I examined his tiny little face, my mind's eye would see the face of a baby of a different race appear on his body. At first I did not understand why that happened when I looked at him but as time passed, my heart knew the answer. What happened to Juan could have happened to any child. I had to find a way to prevent another family from going through my pain.

I could see images of the way he was in my mind and imagined his steps on the day of the accident. The innocence of a child was what my heart and soul wanted so desperately to protect.

I would often sit at his crib and talk to him. I would tell him how God was using him to help other children.

"Juan, don't be afraid. I am here and God is there with you. It's okay to ask God to let you hold His hand. You are his special angel and He has chosen you to fulfill His mission. It is awesome that God chose you. Just remember you have to come back to mommy, I am here with my arms wide open waiting for you. Today is your day for a miracle so you get to the front of the line my baby."

I knew he could hear me, for I could feel it deep in my bones. I would bend down to kiss him and my tears dampened his face.

"God, please give me the strength to do what I have to do to help other children not suffer through what Juan has endured."

Every day that strength became stronger.

Because of my new found strength, I was able to sleep in my bed for the first time in a long time. I tossed and turned the first night but it got easier to be away from him every night. I would set my alarm clock to wake we every 30 to 60 minutes to get up and check on Juan. Most of the time I woke up before the alarm went off. I thank God for watching over him for me.

One night, I had gotten up around 3:00 a.m. to check on him. As I stood at his crib, from the corner of my eye, I saw the end of this white gown go past his door. I quickly turned and there was no one there. I walked into the hallway and found no one there.

Thinking that it was Dereck, I walked into his room to find him asleep. Then I remembered, I had prayed and asked God to place two angels at Juan's door to protect him. My fears went away. I thanked him and went to sleep.

Later, one of the nurses told me she saw the images too, but did not say anything because she did not want to frighten us. She said she too was frightened at first but had gotten used to seeing them and was no longer afraid.

With the holiday being only a few days away, each day was one we truly were grateful to God for. I wished Juan could have been able to enjoy it for it was his first Thanksgiving that he could have eaten from the table. My heart developed peace giving thanks to him being alive and home.

My mother had gone home so that she would be there for the holiday with the rest of the family. She always cooked large meals for Thanksgiving. I told her that we would be okay and to tell everyone I said hello and I wish I could have been home with them for the holiday.

Our Thanksgiving was wonderful. It was the day after that brought forth heartache.

I had gotten up to go and pick up supplies for Juan.

On my way past his room, I stopped and asked the nurse, "Are you going to be okay with Juan being here by yourself? I have to go and pick up some supplies."

"Sure, Ms. Boatwright. You go right ahead, we will be fine," she responded.

I left to go to the drug store. Each step I made, my gut kept telling me that I should go home. Listening to my instincts, I jumped in my car and sped through traffic trying to get home.

As I rushed inside, I could hear the alarms on his machines going off. I dropped my bags at the door and ran inside his room to find the nurse just standing there looking at the machines.

"My God! Why are you not bagging him?" I screamed as I began to bag him to give him oxygen.

"I come from a nursing home background, Ms Boatwright. There we had a DNR and when they started to go, we let them go."

I began to pray, asking God to plant my feet. After bringing his oxygen levels up, I told her to suction his trachea to help clear his airway.

Her sterile technique was awful, the catheter she was about to insert into his trachea had touched her face, the bed, and my arm, making it no longer sterile.

As she began to insert it, I grabbed her hand to stop her. "You don't have a clue as to what you are doing, do you?" I said to her.

"At the nursing home we didn't have sterile technique. I told them that I was not comfortable coming out here, but they told me to just go anyway and if anything happened to call 911," she said.

I showed her the sterile process at least seven times and she was not able to master it.

Being that it was time for his medication, she started to draw up his medicine. I looked and was totally shocked to find the amount that she had drawn up to give him.

"What are you doing?" I asked.

"I am getting his medicine ready," she said.

"Can't you read? The bottle clearly says 2.4mls and you have drawn up 10mls," I told her.

She stuttered through her explanation.

"I know you need the money for your family, so I am going to allow you to complete your shift, but you sit there in that chair until it is time for you to leave. I am going to call your office to find out why they sent you here if they knew you were not capable of taking care of Juan," I said to her.

She went over and sat in the chair apologizing for her lack of knowledge. As her shift neared its end, I called her office. I spoke with the nurse who did the scheduling. I asked her why did she send her to my home, knowing that she was not capable of saving my son's life.

She said. "Ms. Boatwright, I had no idea that she did not know how to do the things she needed to do."

"This woman can't bag or suction, and she told me she told you all that she did not feel comfortable coming here, but you sent her anyway," I said.

"No, Ms. Boatwright, she never told us that and she has worked with other babies on vents," she replied.

"You all better stop sending her out because she is going to kill someone. Do not send her back to my home again," I said, as I hung up the telephone.

My heart sank as the thought of what would have happen, had I not come home when I did. God is truly a merciful God and I thanked Him for sending me home in time.

Later that evening, I walked into Juan's room to find his heart rate at 198 and climbing. I immediately fell to my knees in tears, I feared that God had left me.

"God please don't let me be put to shame for trusting in you and for waiting on you. There is something terribly wrong with my baby and I don't know what it is, please help me to find out," I prayed.

I got up and I began to sing *Come by Here Lord,* as I picked up and straighten his room. I walked into the laundry room and came back to find his heart rate had lowered to around 140 beats. I thanked God for answering my prayer.

Later that night the next nurse came in and I went to bed. She woke me up around 5:00 a.m. that morning.

"Ms Boatwright, Juan's heart rate is really high, I think we should get him to the hospital," she said.

I went into his room. "How are you giving him his medications?" I asked.

"I've never given him medicine," she said.

"But here is his medical sheet that is signed after giving him medicine," I explained.

I took the sheet and upon examination, found that Juan was being overdosed on three medications. Two of which were very dangerous.

"Oh my God! He is over-medicated. They have been giving him 10ml of dilantin!" Dilantin is an anti-seizure medication that if overdosed, could result in death.

I called 911 and requested an ambulance. They had also given him more than prescribed on potassium and colace. I started calling the nurses who had signed off on giving him the overdose of medications.

My first call was to the nurse that did the staff scheduling.

I said to her, "Juan has been overmedicated by your nurses. All of you gave him 10mls dilantin, when the bottle and the doctor's orders clearly said 2.4ml." I heard nothing but complete silence. "Tell me, was 10 ml of dilantin not a red flag to you for a child his age?"

She responded, "No."

I said, "I am asking you again, was that amount of medication for a child his age not a red flag for you?"

Again, she responded, "No."

I asked, "Do you even understand my anger at this point?"

She responded sarcastically, "Those are your feelings I can't tell you how to feel."

I told her that the best thing for her to do at that point was to get me the manager on the telephone immediately and I hung up.

As I went down the list calling each of them, they all had no explanation as to why they were giving him the overdose of medication.

While I spoke with one of the nurses, my call waiting clicked. I hung up and connected to the manager. I expressed how upset I was.

"You promised me that this would not happen to my baby!"

"I don't understand what could have happened. Jackie I promise you these are people I would let take care of my family," she said. This had become her signature line.

"Is 10ml of dilantin a red flag to you for a baby Juan's age?" I asked.

"Well, that depends on the concentration," she responded.

"Where would you find the concentration of a medication?' I asked.

She responded, "On the bottle."

"Well if the dosage is on the bottle and they are not looking at it I find it hard for you to convince me that they would be looking at the concentration!" I shouted.

"Jackie, I promise you these..."

Interrupting her I said, "Please do not tell me that again! You have played on my religious beliefs by pretending to be a Christian. They are not taking care of your family. They are taking care of mine! You need to get me something that can justify why they gave Juan all that medicine!" I said, as I slammed the telephone down.

I sat in the emergency room waiting for the doctor to come in to see about Juan. Finally, he came in. I started to tell him that Juan was over-medicated.

Looking at me as though I had insulted him, he asked. "What makes you think that he is over-medicated?"

I realized that I was the one being insulted.

"Get your calculator out." I said.

He reached into his lab coat pocket and got the calculator.

"This is the doctor's orders, and this is the concentration," I said as I pointed on the bottle showing him. "Does your calculation match the dosage on this bottle according to these orders?"

His face showed a look of intrigue. I then took out Juan's medical record sheet.

"This is what they have been giving him with the exception of the times I gave him medicine."

"How did you learn to calculate medication dosage?" he asked.

"I learned a lot after being in ICU for such a long time," I answered.

He walked away smiling as he ordered blood work on Juan. He later returned with two other doctors.

"This is the mother, I was telling you about. She can calculate medicine." They all seemed shocked that a mother could learn to do something such as that.

Juan was admitted after his blood work showed his dilantin level to be .40, which is two times the safe level.

"Thank you, God," I said silently.

After Juan's dilantin levels had lowered we were told we would be able to go home. Dilantin is the type of medicine that leaves the body rather quickly once you stop giving it, but can be very damaging at high levels when it is in the body.

The thought of going home with them made me sick. I did not want to let them take care of Juan anymore. I knew that I had no choice, because this was the only company in Augusta that took care of children in Juan's condition.

When we arrived home, one of the nurses asked for the medical record sheet. I told her that I left it at the hospital with the doctor.

"We need that back, we need to white that out," she said.

I could not believe I had heard her correctly. I did not respond because I knew that I had the medical sheet.

I didn't know how I was going to sleep not being able to trust the nurses any more. I tried but my dreams became nightmares. I would wake up drenched in sweat and fear. I would race into Juan's room just to make sure that he was okay. I did not know how long I could keep this up. I could feel my body getting weary. Not from taking care of Juan but from watching them to make sure that they did nothing to cause him any further harm.

Each day I would call around trying to find another nursing company that would take Juan's case. I called the hospital social worker and asked her to help me find a new company. I expressed to her my feelings and how my trust in the present company had been damaged.

As Christmas approached, I was so excited, just grateful that my child was alive. I made Juan cassette tapes that contained Christmas songs and prayers. I started playing them for him and he responded to hearing my voice. One of his favorite songs was the *Christmas Song* by Nat King Cole.

I remember when I had taken him to have his picture taken, he was knocking over every prop the photographer put up. I started singing the *Christmas Song* and he just stopped and looked at me until the song was over. We got some beautiful pictures. I would sing that same song when he was into things around the house, and he would always stop whatever he was doing and listen. The key was I had to keep singing it in order to hold his attention.

The Christmas spirit filled me as I decorated the house and put up the tree. I wanted Dereck's Christmas to be a happy one. I only wished I could have gotten him all the things he wanted. He was really showing a lot of courage with all we were going through.

I sat him down and told him, "Sweetheart, mommy is so sorry she can't get you the things you want this year, but I have been put in a difficult situation."

"It's okay, mommy. Juan needs us right now. I understand," he said.

I grabbed him and cried. I could not believe how well he was handling things.

"Don't cry mommy. You are a good mother and I love you," he told me.

"I love you too, baby," I said as I wiped the tears from my face.

A few days later three of my girlfriends came to visit. We all sat around and laughed about old times. They still had a way of making me laugh to the point of tears. I really needed their visit. The nurse watched Juan as we sat at my kitchen table and talked girl talk. My heart felt a little sad when I walked them to the door to say good-bye.

When I got ready for bed, I wished Juan could sleep with me. The way everything had been set up on his cart I could move it to other locations in the house. I don't think it was set up this way with those intentions, but my heart rejoiced that it was. I called Dereck in to help me. I was able to carry Juan as Dereck pulled his cart that held his ventilator.

I laid Juan on my bed. I looked at him and his eyes had opened. I praised God. Juan knew that he was in his bed. I slept close to him all night. We took him back to his room the next morning.

I got so tickled one day, as I looked at the gifts under the tree.

Dereck had torn a small whole in each of his gifts. I called for him to come to me.

"Why did you tear holes into the presents?" I said trying to keep a straight face.

Before he could answer, I burst out into laughter causing him to laugh. I remembered how I did the same thing as a child thinking my mother would never know. We both laughed. I think he needed it, too.

We began to reminisce about things Juan did.

"Mama, I bet Juan would have done turned this tree over by now," he said laughing.

"I know he would have," I responded.

"Remember how we would be watching television and it would be at the good part and all of a sudden the channel would change and you would think I did it and I would think you did it? And it would be Juan with the remote," Dereck said.

"What about the time he hit me in the head with your drum sticks?" I added. We continued for quite some time going down memory lane about Juan.

Christmas was finally here and I was glad. We opened our presents and thanked the Lord. We had our best Christmas ever, for the meaning was totally different.

The New Year would be a new beginning for us. We had somewhat adjusted to Juan's situation. I knew that deep inside, I had to do all I could to help insure other children and their families would not go through what we were going through. This thought consumed me more and more with each passing day.

One day while attempting to balance my checkbook, I realized that I had nothing left to balance. I had given all I had to Juan's medical bills. I kept asking myself, how was I going to take care of my children? All I had was my faith that God would prepare a way for us. Although Satan tried to make me worry, something deep in me would not let me.

I'd written a brief story about Juan and all that God had done for us and I began leaving copies at restaurants and other locations. It contained my telephone number and address.

People began to call and ask if I would pray for them. I often told God that this was too much for me, that I did not feel worthy for something of this magnitude. I allowed those that requested to come to my home and I would pray with them.

I remember a young girl that called me and requested prayer. She told me that she was in a car accident about a year earlier. She said the doctors told her that she was fine, but she keeps having headaches and dizziness. The next day she and her mother came over. I shared with her that it would be according to her faith that her healing would manifest.

We went into Juan's room and prayed. I always felt the presence of the Lord in his room. I know that she was healed. I could feel the Holy Spirit as I prayed to God for her.

How was I going to do this? I was not a perfect person, but for some reason, God had found favor in me. I remembered one of my first encounters when God spoke to me. It was about 10 to 12 years ago. I was living at home. I had just finished exercising on my gym equipment I had set up in my bedroom. I was getting ready to get in the shower. As I walked toward my bathroom, I began to walk backwards, beyond my control. I was laid flat on my back on my bed when I realized that I could not move. I was very aware of all that was happening. I heard this voice call my name repeatedly.

I refused to answer, until the voice finally said, "Jackie, this is Jesus."

"What do you want?" I asked.

"I am going to give you a business, you are going to prosper, but you will have to do something for me.," the voice said.

"What is that?" I asked.

"You have to tell everybody about me."

"I can do that," I said.

"Now you can move," Jesus said. I jumped up and ran outside to share what had happened with my mother. She told me that maybe I was dreaming. I assured her that I was not.

Now I was in a situation where I was telling everybody about Jesus. I had been asked by several churches to tell Juan's Story. God's love for him quickly spread.

Juan had an episode of elevated heart rate that required him to be back in ICU. I tried not to allow this to break my spirits.

One day as I sat watching television in his room, I looked to find a woman standing at his door. I turned down the volume so that I could hear her. She told me about her infant granddaughter who was in the room next to Juan. She said that she was not eating and the doctors did not know why. She also said that her daughter, the mother of the baby, was real torn up about all of this.

She asked me, if I would pray with her. I said yes.

We went to the consultation room where the young lady was. I sat down and began to share with her all that God had done for Juan.

I asked her, "Are you saved?"

She replied, "No."

I told her the importance of her salvation and the healing she wanted for her baby. She nodded her head in understanding.

She asked me, "Will you pray for my baby?"

"Sure I will," I said.

We went back to ICU to the baby's room. We were not able to go in the room, because the doctors were trying to get an IV started on the baby. While we stood outside waiting, I told her that she must listen for the voice of God to speak to her. Quite some time had passed and they still had not gotten the IV in the baby.

I told the young lady that because we could not pray for the baby at this time, she could get saved now. I led her through the scripture of salvation.

It wasn't five minutes later, the doctor walked out into the hallway where we were standing and said, "Thank God, we finally got the IV in her."

I told the young lady that God had just spoken to her. The doctor could not even take credit for getting the IV started. We embraced and I thanked God for doing only what I knew he could have done.

The next day the young lady and I would have several conversations about things she was going through. I shared with her similar situations that I had gone through. I warned her about Satan, and how he was going to come at her, now that she was saved. I told her she needed to be prepared to pray harder than ever before.

Juan was released from the hospital the next day. I told her and her mother to remember all that I shared with them and that everything was going to be all right. For some reason I felt my leaving made her apprehensive about her strength and faith in God. I reassured her of her strength and that God would not leave her alone.

When we got home, it came to me. Juan's heart rate calmed the same day young lady was led to salvation. I often wonder if God sent us to the hospital for that very reason, the young lady and her baby.

Later that week the young lady was constantly on my mind. I called the hospital to inquire how she was doing. I could not remember the baby's name.

After being transferred to several different extensions, I asked the operator transfer me back to the ICU. Juan had been a patient there so many times that all the nurses knew me. I asked her the name of the baby that was in the room next to Juan when he was there a few days ago. She told me the name and transferred me to the fourth floor, where they had been moved. As soon as the young lady answered the telephone, I knew that my telephone call was led by God.

"Jackie, I am so glad you called me. The doctors are saying that they may have to put her back in ICU," she said.

"You listen to me. Satan is trying to test your faith. I am going to hang this telephone up and I want you to pray to God and rebuke him out right now. You were saved according to the word of God. I will call you back in a few minutes," I said.

About twenty or thirty minutes passed and I called her back. Her voice this time projected a sound of true happiness.

"Is everything okay?" I asked.

"Yes, the doctor just walked in and told me that he was not sending her back to ICU." We both praised God.

"See, I told you He is a man of His word," I said.

The baby's ailment turned out to be something simple. She started taking her formula and the family went home.

During another episode when Juan had to go back into ICU, the little girl with cancer was brought back into the unit. After we were released from the hospital, I found out that she lost her battle. I knew that those people had great faith in God. I told myself that she was one of those whose lives had been written with a short number of days.

My calling around for a new nursing company finally paid off. Another pediatric home nursing company had recently opened a branch office in Augusta. I called and they agreed to take Juan's case. I was not expecting any miracles, just some relief from what I was feeling toward the nurses that over-medicated Juan.

When the new company took over, I made it clear about all that I had gone through, and that I was not going to go through that again if I could help it.

Things went okay for the first few weeks. I was totally shocked when one of the nurses questioned the fact that I was giving Juan cereal. I made it clear that he was my child, that he was eating pizza and chicken before his accident and I knew that he could not survive on just formula.

"If you all want to continue with my case, you better realize this is my child and I am going to do anything I can to help him get better. He is going to be fed his cereal and that is the bottom line," I told the case manager.

Juan soon progressed, and was able to tolerate baby food from the jar through his feeding tube. After I had begun to feed him the baby food, I could tell that his strength increased. His blood work was always excellent. His doctor said that everything about a child that makes him grow was working great with Juan. I thanked God for laying on my heart and mind to feed him.

One of the nurses with the new company had a friend who was a nurse and a paramedic. She told me that she had told her about Juan. She said the lady wanted to work with our company and be on Juan's case. I told her sure. I felt if anybody could be an asset, a nurse who was also a paramedic would be wonderful. I considered her coming to be a blessing from God.

A few weeks passed and I asked why she had not come out. The nurse that recommended her did not know. Finally, she came over for me to meet her. Her name was Frances. After her first day of orientation, I told her that she had the job.

During one of her visits, she told me that she heard the initial call when my son's accident happened. She asked if I wanted to know what she had heard over the radio. At first I hesitated, then I asked that she tell me.

"Well when the call came through and we heard it was a baby, you could hear a pin drop in our station. The paramedic that was at the scene was working very hard, but when I heard the drugs she had to give him, I knew he had expired," Frances said.

My heart became full and I cried. Just imagining all that he went through hurt a lot. I knew that no matter what had happened, God had brought him back to me. Hearing her recall that day, hurt on one hand; but it was like medicine to my soul on the other hand.

We grew closer. Her love for Juan was evident. I would later ask her to be his godmother.

One time Frances called me into Juan's room.

"Jackie have you noticed Juan's eyes?" she said.

"What do you mean?" I responded.

"Well, when I look in his eyes, I see eyes looking back at me, but they are not his eyes. It is almost like Jesus is looking at you," she said.

"I know what you mean. I have had my experience with his eyes as well. One time I was holding him and as our eyes met all I could do was cry and repent," I told her.

She went on to tell me of another nurse and her saying something similar happened to her.

Sometimes I would start singing to Juan and before I knew it I would the Holy Spirit will fill the room and my praises to God would be all you could hear. It was the most awesome feeling to have the spirit of God take over my body, mind and soul.

My friends had begun to wonder about my social life, thinking that I was not taking time for me. I really had not thought about the fact of my social life. I was having a great time taking care of Juan. I was somewhat of a home-body anyway, so I was comfortable with being home.

To take you to a lighter side of this story: All of my girlfriends had the perfect man for me. We would spend time laughing because they were never able to match me with anyone that I liked. But the time we spent trying to find Mr. Right was so much fun, for my joy came more from the presence of my friends than their attempts to get me hitched. I kept telling them that God would take care of that part, too.

I remember one of them saying. "Girl, God has so much to do let us give him a little help."

Their craziness brought laughter from deep within.

I used to tease one of my single girlfriends, "Girl we are never going to find a man who is going to put up with our being so head-strong and outspoken."

She would always give the same answer each time I would say this, "I am not going to claim that. God is going to send me my man."

I would laugh and say, "I know he is and you know I was just kidding."

We would always burst into laughter as she would sum it up by saying, "Girl, you better stop saying that before God hears you."

I truly thank God for those who stuck by me throughout this ordeal. I prayed that God would bless them for doing so.

My plight to help other children led me to the issue of liability insurance requirements for state licensed child daycare centers. The center where Juan stayed had no liability insurance, therefore, there was no recourse for the injury he sustained. I knew that I must get this information out to other parents. They needed to be aware that there was no legal requirement for insurance, and there was strong possibility that the daycare facility their child was uninsured.

I called one of the local TV stations and asked to speak with a reporter. The secretary transferred me to the reporter. He was excited about the story, as well as totally unaware that there was no state law requiring child daycare centers to have liability insurance.

The reporter came to my home and did the interview. During the taping, I became overwhelmed as I recalled what happened on September 9, 2001, and we had to stop the taping for me to regain my composure.

In his story, he had interviewed one of our local state representatives. I had previously shared with her my son's story, and what I wanted to see done to help other children and families, who might find themselves in similar situations. The last time we talked, she shared with me that she was afraid that it would be difficult to convince her fellow lawmakers on this issue. I could not understand why she would think that would difficult to convince the lawmakers, when we were talking about children.

As the weeks passed, I kept calling trying to get any lawmaker I could to listen to what I was saying. I realized that this was not a local issue; it affected our state.

I called Information and requested the names and numbers for state representatives in other cities. My next call went to Savannah, Georgia. I spoke with a senator and briefly told him my story and asked if he would allow me to come to his office and meet with him. He agreed. I then placed calls to the media in that area to let them know my story and they all requested interviews on my visit to Savannah.

I knew that I needed to go to Savannah, but in all honesty, the thought of being that far away from Juan scared me. What would I do if something happened to Juan? How would I get back home quick enough to be with him? I had prayed to God for his safety as I took this trip. In a brief flash in my mind, I almost wished he were in the hospital so that I knew he would be where he needed to be if something happened.

The day before my trip to Savannah, June 6th. I was at work and called home to check on Juan.

The nurse answered and said, "He is doing fine. He is sitting up in his chair"

Within a few minutes, I heard his machines go off in the background. I knew all of those sounds too well.

"His oxygen levels are dropping, you need to bag him." I said nervously.

"Oh my God, call 911!" She screamed.

"Oh God, please help him." I prayed.

"I don't care what you do, don't stop bagging him!" I said to her.

I attempted to dial 911 from the telephone at work, but all I got was that city's 911.

I then called the sheriff's office in Augusta and told them, "My baby is on a ventilator, he is in respiratory distress, please get an ambulance to my house now! I live at 2572 Lincolnton Parkway. Please get someone out there to help my baby," I said.

I also called Juan's nursing company, and asked the case manager to call 911. I ran from the building, quickly locking the door behind me. I was forty-five minutes away from home. I turned my emergency flashers on and sped off. I was suddenly taken back to September 9th.

I started calling my family members, sobbing trying to explain as best I knew how, that something had happened to Juan. I called my home again, there was no answer. I hurt all over.

I began to kick and scream, "God please don't take my baby, you promised."

I called Frances on her cellular telephone, I knew she was a paramedic and she would know what was going on with Juan.

"I am in route, they are taking him to Eisenhower," she said.

"Is he alive, Frances?" She did not respond.

I screamed to the top of my lungs, releasing all of my pain. Then there was this sense of peace that came over me.

"What if you have an accident and hurt yourself. Juan is in God's hands, and there is nothing at this point that you can do," I heard this voice say.

I slowed the speed of my car, and I started to talk to God in the same peace he had all of sudden showered on me. I drove to Eisenhower not knowing if Juan was alive, but at peace with myself.

As I neared the military base, my telephone rang it was Frances.

"He is okay. He has a heart beat," she said. I was elated.

They sent a police escort to lead me to the hospital. I walked in and found Juan surrounded by doctors and nurses. Many of them were there on September 9th and remembered him.

The ambulance transported him back to the Children's Medical Center once he was stable. My prayer was answered. It wasn't necessarily the way I would have preferred, but Juan was in the hospital when I went to Savannah. I knew that Satan was doing all that he could to stop me from making the trip. God protected us, and again reminded me that he had not left us.

When my attorney and I arrived, the reporter had interviewed the senator on the issue. I feel safe to say that those I had come in contact with thought as I had in regard to insurance; we assumed they had to have it in order to have a state license.

They all began to tell me how courageous I was for doing this. I did not feel courageous, I felt as a mother, I had to do something so that Juan's injury was not in vain. I did not want what had happened to him to disappear like dust in the wind. Even more, I knew I was on a mission for God.

The Senator favored my request for liability enforcement on state licensed child day care centers in Georgia. I did interviews with all the television stations in Savannah. I was overjoyed, that somebody listened to me.

I contacted Greg, the newspaper reporter, and asked him to come out and allow me to share with him my desire to see a new law implemented to require state licensed daycare centers to have liability insurance. He said he wanted to cover it in the newspaper. The story prompted several telephone calls from local citizens commending me and offering any assistance they could with what I was going through. I could not take credit for my strength, I had to give credit to God..

A few weeks later, I received a letter from the Governor. I had written to him not really expecting a response. I opened the letter and was totally touched by his sincerity, and the fact that he addressed Juan by name. In his letter, he arranged a meeting between the Commissioner who headed the Child Licensing Division and me, in Atlanta, Georgia.

Prior to going to Atlanta, Juan celebrated his second birthday, and I thanked God for this milestone. I knew that it was the grace of God, that he made it to this day. We celebrated with a program and dinner at our church in the town where I grew up. Juan was provided an ambulance for the day to transport him on the fifty-mile trip.

So many of our friends and family members showed up to help us celebrate this remarkable day. I presented plaques to the firefighters and 911 personnel for their roles in saving Juan's life. I could tell that many were amazed that Juan had lived as long as he had considering the injury he suffered. God had truly found favor in us.

My mother came and stayed with Juan as I went to Atlanta for the meeting.

When I walked into the Commissioner's office, he extended his hand and said, "I want you to know that I agree with you. Child day care centers in Georgia should be insured." I felt pleased to know this.

Unknown to me the Licensing Director for Department of Human Resources was also present. He introduced himself to me. I could tell by his responses that he was not keen on the idea of enforcing insurance on day cares.

"You know, the parents are not going to like the idea of the cost of daycare going up if there is enforcement of insurance," he said.

"Well, I'd like for you to ask any parent to exchange places with me for one hour," I responded.

He got quiet. For some reason, he was never able to look directly at me. The Commissioner asked that he go down the list of states that do require liability insurance on state licensed day cares.

"I am sure you already have done a lot of research on this, Ms. Boatwright, you seem very knowledgeable on the issue," he said.

"Yes, I have and I am familiar with the fact that there are about 22 states that do not require liability insurance. Georgia does not need to be on that list. We need to be on the insured list," I responded.

"Sure we do," the Commissioner said.

After the Director finished the list he said, "The cost for insurance is going to be very high, and some smaller day cares are not going to be able to afford insurance."

"If they can't afford it sir, maybe they don't need to be in business. We are talking about children, not someone repairing your roof incorrectly or installing a plumbing fixture wrong. Millions of parents opt to use day care everyday in order to provide a living for their families. We need to make sure the operators are accountable if a child is injured, and the only way to do that, is by enforcing insurance. When I saw that state license, I automatically assumed there was insurance. Can you imagine the number of parents that are just like me? We leave our children, and we walk out of the door with the sense of security after seeing a state issued license. The state license means so much more to a parent, than someone who does not have a license. We have to protect the children," I said.

At that point, the Commissioner asked, "Are you supposed to meet with some of the representatives at the capitol?"

"Yes," I responded.

"Tell them that if they need any assistance in writing the bill to let me know," he said. I silently praised God as I thanked him.

After our meeting was complete, he had his assistant drive me over to the capitol where I met with Representative Brooks. He assured me that the bill was going to be written and on the floor of the House during the 2003 general assembly.

On my way home, I called the television stations in Augusta to share the good news. They were eagerly waiting to hear how my meeting in Atlanta turned out. I was at that moment one of the happiest women in the world. I really felt I had almost won my battle.

I returned home to find Juan was doing great. I was glad that my mother was there with him. She listened to the details of my trip with as much as excitement as I had telling her. She told me the local news aired clips of my visit several times throughout the day while I was in Atlanta.

"You know Mom, I never told you how much it helped me when you told me to take this thing all the way," I said.

"I know how much this means to you and I want you to know I am proud of you," she said.

I went on to share with her about a dream I had one night, of being invited to take a tour, of the "most beautiful cemetery in the world." In my dream, I walked through the cemetery, in awe at how beautiful it was. All the graves were those of babies. Some of the graves had twins, triplets and even quadruplets. I remember walking out, but not much more after that.

Another dream involved seeing a baby in a casket. The face on the baby was Juan's. I awoke drenched in sweat. I ran into his room, and saw that he was okay. I could not hold back my tears as I bent down, held him and wept. A few hours later I received a telephone call, the baby that was at the end of the hall when Juan was first at ICU had died. I hurt for the mother. I reflected on her dreams of Juan and her baby waking up at the same time. I must say that I was a bit frightened. I prayed to God to give me strength to endure through this tragedy. He did.

In another dream, my telephone rang. When I answered, it was Robin on the other end. She asked me how I was doing and began to talk about old times. I remember crying and thinking that she did not realize she was dead. But her laughter was joyful and in my dream, I stopped crying and started laughing with her because I knew she was in heaven. I do believe only heaven can bring the joy I could hear in her voice.

I had received a letter from Richard about the second hearing date in the case against Maria. I filed suit against her to show the devastation a situation like mine could cause a family.

I was very hesitant about going back to trial because during the first hearing the Judge seemed to show no compassion for my baby. Before the clerk called my case in front of the judge, I sat in the courtroom for more than an hour listening to an argument about a zoning map.

Maria did not show up for court. When our turn came, and Richard attempted to abreast him of our case, the judge began to wave his hands as though we were wasting his time.

"You don't have to go tell me all that, I can read," he said in a sarcastic tone. My stomach wrenched.

"What's the purpose of this lawsuit? What state of being is the child in?" he blurted.

As Juan's pediatrician was asked to respond, my emotions took over. I listened as he gave the number of years Juan would live, and the quality of life he would have.

I gasped, as the contents of my stomach raced toward my throat. Tears streamed down my face, as I turned to Richard. He felt my pain, and gave me his look of encouragement not to run. I sat there unable to control my silent cries until he dismissed the case asking both attorney's to return with case law on timeliness of filing court motions.

I stood out in the hallway and waited for Richard to come out of the courtroom.

Maria's attorney approached me. "I am very sorry for what happened to your son, Ms. Boatwright. I am a parent, too. I just wanted you to know that."

My deepest thoughts were to slap his face; instead, my quick prayers provided me the ability to nod my head in acceptance of his remark.

Richard and I stood in front of the courthouse building waiting for the television reporter to get set up for an interview.

"I can't do this interview, Richard," I said to him.

"I understand, I'll take care of it," he responded.

I walked away still feeling the pain from the hearing. I saw two men carrying a cross in front of the court house building. I approached them and asked the meaning of what they were doing.

They began to explain that they were protesting, one of them asked, "Why are you crying?"

I shared with them Juan's story. They were familiar with it after reading the many articles from the paper. I sobbed as they prayed to God for me and for Juan.

During the next hearing, Richard provided the judge with a copy of the case law about time limits on filing motions. The other attorney did not have a case to present to the judge.

I thought maybe the judge's demeanor would have changed, since the last time we appeared before him. I was wrong. This time God had given me the strength to look directly at him.

I guess he saw on my face, the hurt he was causing me as he began to explain, "Ms. Boatwright, I don't want you to think I have no compassion for your baby, because I do. I also want to commend you for all you are doing to get a law passed requiring daycare centers to be insured. They need to have insurance."

"Thank you," I said.

As the hearing proceeded, Richard asked if I could address the court. The judge placed me under oath and allowed me to speak.

"There is no amount of money you can give me today that would replace the life of my child, and all he has endured. I know that you are wondering because of his condition, what is purpose of a lawsuit? His condition should not take away from what he is legally and rightfully owed for his suffering due to the negligence of someone else.

"Juan is not brain dead. He opens his eyes. He cries real tears. When he is given his baby shots at his pediatrician's office, he pulls away in pain and has to be held as a normal child does. He makes noises and attempts to talk. He can move his arms and legs. He also can stay off his ventilator for about 2 hours some times breathing on his own.

"I believe in my heart he is going to get up. He is making a lot of progress. It is just going to take some time. I have a right to hold on to that hope. I pray the court will award him what he is entitled," I said with a tearful tremble in my voice.

The judge ruled the case in my favor and said he would make an award amount when Richard presented him with additional information from Juan's doctor. I told Richard that I could not assist him with getting the information, because I could not bear to hear someone put a number on Juan's life. He understood and agreed to handle it on my behalf.

As I started writing this book, God let me know that he was not through with me. I had called a friend of mine, who told me a high school classmate of hers was in the hospital. He was in a four wheeler accident, and was in ICU in a coma. She said, she told the family about the young man on the fourth floor, who I had prayed for. She also told them how the doctors had given up on him, but through prayer, he walked out of the hospital.

The Holy Spirit led me to visit her friend in the hospital. As I was led by his sisters to ICU where he laid comatose. I read the fifth chapter of the book of James. I anointed his head and began to pray.

The minister told the family that the man could not receive salvation, because he could not respond. I believed that comatose patients could hear those around them. I told the man if he could hear me, to talk to God in his mind. I asked God to listen to his mind because even if he could respond, with all of the tubes in his throat he wouldn't be able to do so. I began to intercede to God on his behalf. I recited the scripture of salvation.

Just as my prayer ended, the man opened his eyes. His family was in shock as tears streamed their faces.

"He's awake!" one of them said.

I asked him, "Did you receive the scripture of salvation?"

He nodded his head yes. I praised God as I shared in their excitement.

As I was about to leave, they led me down the hall to another waiting room. They introduced me to a family whose daughter had been in a bad automobile accident. The victim's sister led me to ICU to pray for her. Their mother was at her side, she was heavily sedated and on a ventilator due to damage to her lungs from the accident. I could feel the presence of God the moment I walked in the room.

I began to pray and the Holy Spirit took over, speaking directly to God in tongues. A few weeks thereafter, she was released from the hospital to go home.

So that you know, I do not think or feel I have any special powers. I do believe that God has found favor in me and has chosen me as a vessel to show His Self.

The book of Mark chapter 16 verses 15-18 says, *"And He said unto them, Go ye into all the world, and preach the gospel to every creature. He that believeth and is baptized shall be saved; but he that believeth not shall be damned. And these things shall follow them that believe; In My name shall they cast out devils; they shall speak with new tongues; they shall take up serpents and if they drink any deadly thing, it shall not hurt them; they shall lay hands on the sick, and they shall recover."*

It has been through my faith in God, that Juan is still alive and that the people who I prayed for have been healed, nothing that I have done, can do or ever will be able to do.

I believe in the word of God with my whole heart. There are times when I get afraid. It is in those times, when I truly look upon my faith to get me through.

So many have asked me, where does my strength come from. My answer will always be the same, God. He will never put more on you than you can bear if you trust him.

I trust God and I constantly remind him of his promises. I could have never imagined God using me and to this day I am still puzzled but I am also grateful that God sees my heart.

Many I have met have a tremendous amount of faith but they lack the ability to stand on that faith in their darkest hours. It is when you can stand the test, when it seems there is no hope or no way out of a situation, when God will open the windows of heaven and your miracles will manifest.

Juan's life is because of my faith in God's promises. Everybody that Jesus healed, received the healing because of their faith in what they were asking God to do. Lazarus was raised from the dead, because his family *believed* that if Jesus would have been there, he would not have died. The woman with the issue of blood was healed, because she *believed* if she could just touch the hem of His garment, she would be made whole. It was faith that brought Abraham, Moses, Daniel and the Hebrew Boys through their situations.

I had to learn that God works in his own timing. I am forever reminded of the old adage, whatever is worth having is worth waiting for. Well use that when you ask God for whatever you may need and wait on Him to give it to you.

I just emailed the President of the United States…….

Embracing Life

Being an African American Female Entrepreneur has been both fulfilling and rewarding. I have not only brought so much into what I have gained throughout my life and work experiences but I have gained in two folds much more. Being in the business of fitness has allowed me the opportunity to share the greatest gift I think that God could have allowed me to share; and that is the gift of healthy living. I can honestly say that my decision to open my business in my hometown was the best choice I could have made. I am surrounded by so many who have been instrumental in shaping and molding me as to who I am today.

The women that I am about to speak of, you may not know, but I hope you can feel their spirit as told through me.

I am forever amazed and uplifted by all of my former grade school teachers, who have taught me the real meaning to the term "embracing life." Each in her own unique style, has shown me just how I should live my life.

I will start Ellen Douglas, a woman in her seventies, is the epitome of beauty and class. Each day she visits the fitness center she has her dynamic smile all across her face. As the music plays throughout the room, I am in full laughter as she snaps her fingers and "cuts a few steps to the beat." She has taught me how and why to dance. So now as the music plays, for the first time I dance, but for a different reason, and all I can tell you is that it feels good. I watch her and it is as if when she dances she goes back in time and thinks of all the good things that God has blessed her with throughout her life and her dances symbolizes so much. Thank you Mrs. Douglas; for teaching me how and why I should dance.

I now move on to Runnette Herrmann. A woman that by watching her eyes, as they light up as though they are high beams on a foggy night; has taught me that beauty, sex appeal, and crazy laughter knows no age limit. She too in her seventies exemplifies that it is okay to feel beautiful, walk beautiful and even more; just be beautiful. Her demeanor personifies self-love in every sense of the word. Thank you Ms. Herrmann, for teaching me how to love myself first, above all things on earth.

Now, a businesswoman, quiet in spirit, with a heart that jumps right out and grabs you, is Vivian Davis. Although I did not have her teach me personally in grade school, she certainly has given me the lesson of a lifetime. Her caring and motherly spirit has taught me how to share myself with others. The warmth of her smile allows you to see the enormous size of her heart. The friendship she shares with Runnette Herrmann, is an extraordinary one whom only women of great character can share. Thank you Ms. Davis, for teaching me how to love others as I love myself.

Last but certainly not least, Harriett Lewis, has shown me I can be beautiful and strong. This woman in her late sixties strives to master every physical task that I as her trainer has put forth to her. I have watched her challenge herself and accomplish each goal. Her eagerness and strong desire to do more has taught me that I can do all and be all, if I just keep at it. Thanks Ms. Lewis for teaching me not to fear what in my heart and soul I know I can do.

All four of these women, all whom have shared "their stories" with me: From surviving breast cancer, not bearing children yet wanting a house full, to the loss of husbands. Throughout all of this, I watched them laugh, dance, and embrace life. Although they are all now retired, they still are great teachers: At least in my eyes.

As a young woman, I often find myself caught up in what I don't have and overlooking what I do have. Through their spirits, I have realized that my happiness depends on how much I dance, smile, love me and love others. I will embrace my life and appreciate every second of every day. I will walk proud, and stand proud as the woman I was born, and have now learned to be.

I truly believe that one is not born with great character, but it is something that over time is learned throughout the lives of those that were before you. If you can find your character as I have in these women and many others. You too will learn to embrace your life, you will learn to dance, to smile and to love. Look around at those that were before you and learn your character, even more learn to embrace your life.